OECD Public Governance Reviews

Engaging Public Employees for a High-performing Civil Service

This work is published under the responsibility of the Secretary-General of the OECD. The opinions expressed and arguments employed herein do not necessarily reflect the official views of OECD member countries.

This document and any map included herein are without prejudice to the status of or sovereignty over any territory, to the delimitation of international frontiers and boundaries and to the name of any territory, city or area.

Please cite this publication as:
OECD (2016), *Engaging Public Employees for a High-performing Civil Service*, OECD Public Governance Reviews, OECD Publishing, Paris.
http://dx.doi.org/10.1787/9789264267190-en

ISBN 978-92-64-26718-3 (print)
ISBN 978-92-64-26719-0 (PDF)

Series: OECD Public Governance Reviews
ISSN 2219-0406 (print)
ISSN 2219-0414 (online)

The statistical data for Israel are supplied by and under the responsibility of the relevant Israeli authorities. The use of such data by the OECD is without prejudice to the status of the Golan Heights, East Jerusalem and Israeli settlements in the West Bank under the terms of international law.

Photo credits: Cover © Colorlife/Shutterstock.com.

Corrigenda to OECD publications may be found on line at: *www.oecd.org/about/publishing/corrigenda.htm*.

Foreword

This report was prepared by the OECD Public Governance and Territorial Development Directorate (GOV), under the direction of Rolf Alter, It is based upon a 2014 Survey conducted by the OECD Public Employment and Management Working Party (PEM) and its related work on employee engagement.

PEM is a collaborative international forum of senior practitioners seeking to address current challenges affecting public services and civil service reform. It undertakes comparative analysis on issues related to strategic civil service management and compensation, which provides governments with unique data to inform reform agendas. The network is one of the main contributors to key GOV projects, such as Government at a Glance.

Engaging public employees for a high-performing civil service publication draws upon the current priorities in public service management across OECD countries. It takes a look at the effects of human resource management (HRM) related cost cutting measures implemented in civil services between 2008 and 2013. Additionally, it explores how some countries are seeking to manage the impacts of such actions by measuring and managing employee engagement to boost performance.

Both parts of this book have been shared and discussed with members of PEM as individual reports and as part of the programme of work of PEM and the Public Governance Committee (PGC). Chapter 2 is based on a report written by Christoph Demmke (Zeppelin University); Chapter 3 is based on a report written by Beatrix Behrens (Geman Employment Agency, Budesagentur für Arbeit). We wish to thank Dr. David Guest (King's College London), Liz Mckeown and Matt Kerlogue (UK), Dustin Brown and Rob Seidner (USA), Orlaigh Quinn (Ireland), Merle Nurmoja (Estonia), Philippe Vermeulen (Belgium), and Wendy de Letter (Flanders Regional Government), who contributed material, and shared useful advice and comments on the book.

In the OECD Secretariat, this report was managed by Daniel Gerson (PEM Project Manager), under the guidance of Edwin Lau (Head of the Reform of the Public Sector RPS Divison). We wish to thank Luiz De Mello (Deputy Director of GOV), Zsuzsanna Lonti (Senior Project Manager) and Stéphane Jacobzone (Deputy Head of RPS Divison) who have given valuable guidance and advice on the report and survey. Useful comments were also provided by Cristina Mendes.

Editorial and production support given by Kate Lancaster, Catherine Roch, Andrea Uhrhammer, Liz Zachary and Lynda Hawe is gratefully acknowledged.

Table of contents

Figures

Boxes

Tables

Tables

Executive summary

Civil services operate during very challenging times. civil servants face complex policy problems, as they are faced with higher citizen expectations, yet, they have fewer resources.

New ways of resolving these dilemmas are needed. Public administrations must attract, recruit, develop and motivate high-calibre employees even during times of budgetary constraint. This requires effective public sector leadership, modern evidence-based reform strategies, and human resource management (HRM) that takes employees' views and expectations into account.

This report takes stock of the HRM cost-cutting measures that were implemented in OECD countries in the wake of the 2008 global financial crisis. It argues that, while cost-control measures may have been necessary, they may also have had unintended effects on workforce performance, motivation and longer term work capacities. Ensuring adequate civil service capacity requires HRM reforms that target productivity and performance, rather than simply cost controls. Public employers need the right people for the right tasks, and, to achieve this, must position themselves as employers of choice in order to recruit, retain, and motivate high-quality talent.

Becoming employers of choice requires reforms that take into account the needs and expectations of an increasingly diverse workforce. To achieve this, a number of OECD countries use regular employee surveys to benchmark and improve organisational performance, leadership and workplace quality from the employee's perspective.

This report first looks at recent OECD research that suggests changes to HRM between 2008 and 2013. These have been driven first and foremost by a reactive need to cut workforce costs, rather than building longer-term workforce capacity and innovation. It then examines the use of employee surveys and employee engagement to address some of these shortcomings.

The OECD survey on HRM cost-cutting between 2008 and 2013 highlights the following findings:

- The majority of OECD countries have been implementing measures to reduce the size of their central public administration.
- Compensation has been reduced and/or frozen in 75% of countries.
- Investments in training were cut in 62% of countries.

The implications of these reforms on civil servants' work intensity, stress, behaviour, and attitudes were also assessed. The survey shows that:

- Overall, there is a significant trend showing more job intensity and more stress in the workplace.

- An important number of OECD countries report a decrease in employees' trust in their organisations and with their leadership, with lower job satisfaction, and a decrease in workplace commitment.
- However, negative behavioural outcomes, such as unethical behaviour, inappropriate use of resources and corruption, were not observed, suggesting that public sector values and ethos play an important role in governing behaviour.

These results illustrate the double challenge facing civil services: reducing size and cost while still attracting and retaining high-calibre talent. Addressing this challenge requires HRM policies that look at people, not just at employment numbers.

The second part of this report, helps address this challenge by exploring the experiences of a number of OECD countries, that have used employee surveys to measure and monitor employee engagement (that is, employees willingness and ability to invest themselves and their work in the organisation's goals). Engagement is empirically linked to better job performance, organisational commitment, productivity and public sector innovation. Improving employee engagement should, therefore, result in improvements in functioning of government.

Measuring engagement can provide a proxy for the performance of management, leadership and HRM systems. Some countries have developed complex benchmarking approaches that enable the comparison of a range of survey scores down to unit levels to compare perceptions, identify areas of excellence and underperformance, and target management interventions. Such surveys thus provide a data-driven, evidence-based tool for improving management decision making and HRM policy development, while creating the basis for sustainable reforms that recognise the central value of the people who make up the public administration.

While the knowledge base for evidence-driven HRM is still young, this report presents some good practices and strategies for addressing and improving engagement:

- Regular employee surveys to measure and benchmark engagement and its drivers.
- Customised reports for managers that benchmark their units' scores against similar units, their organisation, and the civil service average.
- Follow-up processes to develop action plans endorsed by individual managers, with support from engagement specialists in central units (e.g. HRM authority). To be successful, such plans generally need to include:
  - Clear and transparent commitment and accountability from the top leadership of the organisation.
  - Good two-way communication between employees and management through multiple channels.
  - Meaningful opportunities for employees to contribute to workplace improvements.
  - Support to managers to develop action plans that improve their relationship with their employees.
  - HRM policies, strategies and tools which support employee wellbeing, development and performance at all stages of the career-cycle.

By focusing on aligning objectives, practices and strategies attentive to engagement this can also help clarify the changing challenges and pressures faced by the public sector, and how public employees and organisations respond to them. This helps build ownership for some of the difficult decisions that will have to be made and supports more agile and tailored HRM measures.

Chapter 1.

From crisis to performance: Current trends and challenges in public employment

This chapter presents some of the concepts and links the findings from the in-depth analysis of the next two chapters. It describes how most OECD public administrations have been approaching civil service reform to respond to complex policy challenges and to budgetary pressures. It presents two types of HRM measures: cost control measures which look at the workforce in terms of numbers and costs, and reforms primarily intended to maintain the commitment and motivation of employees in the face of difficult retrenchment programmes. It argues that a balance of each is required to manage costs while maintaining longer-term capacity, and introduces the concept of employee engagement as one way of measuring and managing civil service reform.

Civil service management in challenging times

Today's public administrations face policy challenges that are increasingly intertwined, cross-jurisdictional, and less predictable. Globalisation, technology, ageing populations and the shifting values of an increasingly diverse population are some of the trends that impact the capacity of public administrations to keep pace with the needs of the citizens they serve. This fast-changing world requires organisations and their workforces to be flexible and open to change. They are also expected to innovate and use a diverse range of competencies to meet citizens' expectations, and to promote increasingly tailor-made solutions for citizens and other stakeholders. Furthermore, public administrations have a democratic and ethical function to serve the society and the law, protect the population, and function in a sustainable manner.

In this sense, government employment frameworks in OECD countries are very ambitious. They want employment systems that guarantee the observation of fundamental values and administrative law principles, and that ensure a focus on performance, effectiveness, efficiency, integrity and accountability. They are also expected to ensure equal treatment and fairness, and make their employment structures more diversified and representative of the population, while ensuring the merit principle, the equality of chances and the principle of non-discrimination. To attract the best candidates, governments are seeking to be more attractive and competitive compared to private sector policies; however, they must prudently manage taxpayers' money and reward individual performance.

Since 2008, the difficult economic and fiscal situation in most OECD countries has added another layer of complexity to the list of challenges above. Most OECD countries are contemplating different ways of managing people to address tensions in the current socio-economic context:

- Governments need to balance budgetary constraints with the need to have productive, satisfied, innovative and high performing employees.
- Organisations are required to address workforce costs while maintaining and build trust and legitimacy amongst the workforce to ensure the commitment and motivation of their employees.
- Human resource management (HRM) is about the need to be both a cultural guardian and an architect of a new culture (Ulrich, 1997).

The OECD survey profiled in Chapter 2 of this publication shows that between 2008 and 2013, countries implemented many cost-reduction measures in HRM and public employment systems of OECD countries' central public administrations (CPAs). While many of these measures were necessary in the wake of the 2008 financial crisis, there is evidence that they have resulted in a loss of trust, commitment and motivation at the employee level, as well as increased stress in the workplace. If left unchecked, this potentially threatens government effectiveness by undermining worker productivity and contribution to innovation. In many countries with high budgetary pressures, these unintended consequences risk increasing the probability of conflict, decrease the prospects for innovation by consensus, and complicate the processes for building and maintaining support for administrative systems and democratic processes.

Cost cutting measures and reforms in human resource management

In the OECD, there is a sense that change is necessary, and that the measures implemented in the wake of the 2008 crisis are not temporary, but define a new normal. Many public administrations are therefore searching for innovative ways to respond to budgetary pressures, while continually improving services to citizens and increasing productivity in order to win back confidence and trust in areas where they have been lost. This emphasises the competencies and experience of personnel as essential factors for success, and many OECD countries are looking for the right mix of HRM reforms to boost performance while addressing cost concerns. Some countries are managing budgetary constraints while maintaining job satisfaction and job commitment through a focus on HRM and leadership tools to measure and manage employee engagement.

Teague and Roche (2014) distinguish between two types of HRM measures:

- Cost control measures that include the reduction of personnel, pay reductions, recruitment freezes, savings in training policies, short-time working, temporary lay-offs, furloughs, incentivised sabbaticals and voluntary departures, reducing contract or agency employment, and pension cuts. This approach tends to look at the workforce in terms of numbers and costs, with a view to identifying the right number and the acceptable cost.
- Reforms primarily intended to ensure that the motivation and commitment of employees are retained in otherwise difficult retrenchment programmes. These include employee and union engagement measures, and competency development. This approach to HRM reform, when done well, recognises the human element of workforce management: that no two people bring the same abilities and motivations to their work, and that, therefore, the question is not only how many and at what cost, but also which ones supported in which ways to contribute their most and best.

This report argues that although cost control measures may have been necessary to react to unforeseen fiscal crises, HRM reforms should ultimately be undertaken to ensure longer-term capacity, productivity and performance. This means ensuring that the workforce continues to build capability and be motivated to contribute to the effectiveness of their organisation. Looking beyond immediate pressures for consolidation, increasingly complex and "wicked" modern governance challenges still require public administrations to position themselves as employers of choice in order to recruit, retain and motivate high quality talent.

To address such challenges, public administrations need employees who not only identify strongly with their job tasks as contributors to public value, but who also identify strongly with their employer and its organisational goals. Good leadership and the right HRM and employment policies can be the foundation of shaping a culture that is open to innovation and can promote sustainable change, even during times of budgetary pressure. This suggests a need to develop evidence-based reform strategies that take into account the needs and expectations of a diverse and, in many countries, ageing workforce, and that promote work engagement.

Employee engagement and evidence-based leadership

Developing an evidence base is being done increasingly through the use of regular civil service-wide employee surveys that measure and compare employee's perceptions of their work, their organisation, and their leadership. Work engagement (or employee engagement) is a construct that brings these themes together. Engagement is a concept that includes an employee's willingness and ability to invest themselves and their work in their organisation's goals. Engaged employees are those who are "committed to their organisation's goals and values, motivated to contribute to organisational success, and are able at the same time to enhance their own sense of well-being." (MacLeod and Clarke, 2009, 9) Engaged employees are critical for successfully managing change in the public administration, enhancing service orientation, and ensuring customer satisfaction.

Employee engagement, is empirically linked to better organisational outcomes, such as efficiency, productivity, public sector innovation, citizen trust in public sector institutions, and employee trust in organisational leadership. Employee engagement strengthens organisational capacity as it is positively related to individual performance and employee retention. Furthermore, the use of employee surveys provides rich data to benchmark organisations' performance, inform management decision making, and help set reform priorities and strategy. Chapter 3 shows how some countries are using employee surveys to measure engagement to support a more evidence-based view of organisational health, leadership and HRM, and produce better HRM policies and management interventions.

While it is early days for the kind of evidence-driven HRM that is presented and promoted in this report, some common practices can be synthesized from the cases and the literature that appear to have promising results.

The leading practices in the area of engagement are based on regular employee surveys with the following features:

- Regular employee surveys, open to all employees, which are designed around an engagement model/theory, to measure engagement and its drivers. Surveys are generally cross-departmental and civil-service wide, to enable comparative analysis and benchmarking across and within organisations. Conducting the survey at regular intervals enables trends analysis, which is essential to maintain accountability and detect improvements over time.
- Custom reports to managers benchmarking their unit's scores against similar units, their organisation, and the civil service average. These reports enable the manager to see year-over-year trends, and to locate their score within a broader context. It is also important that benchmarks are produced for key performance indicators (KPIs, e.g. engagement index) and contextual factors that may influence the KPI to give indications of follow up mechanisms.

Surveys alone are rarely enough to drive change. Follow-up processes are generally owned by the individual managers, with some centralised specialist support. It is important that each manager accepts the responsibility to respond to their survey scores. Successful responses profiled in chapter 3 that have led to an improvement of scores generally appear to have the following components:

- **Clear commitment from the top leadership of the organisation**. Top leadership clearly communicates to all staff that engagement is a priority, that survey results will be used to make changes, and that later surveys will be used to hold leadership accountable for delivering results.

- **Improved communication**. Whether in the form of face-to-face town hall meetings and/or online social networks, organisations who have successfully improved their engagement scores appear to have developed multiple channels for staff to communicate with senior managers, and vice versa.
- **Meaningful contribution to improvements**. Most successful organisations have put into place processes that enable staff to actively contribute ideas to the improvement of their workplaces and organisational culture.
- **Support to managers**. Direct (e.g. line or middle) managers are a fundamental and sometimes forgotten piece of the puzzle. Managers can benefit from initial support from the survey authority to understand and interpret their results. The quality of the personal relationship between employees and their direct supervisors appears to have a significant impact on engagement. Successful organisations have supported middle managers to develop action plans that improve these relationships. Support could come in the form of toolkits, including HRM tools to negotiate working conditions, learning and development opportunities, and flexible arrangements that fit with individual employees' own needs and ambitions.
- **Holistic and forward looking HRM policies, strategies and tools**. HRM needs to contribute more than HR transactions, numbers analysis and cost control. HRM policies can support employee wellbeing, development and performance at all stages of a lifecycle. HRM tools can support managers and leaders to ensure they are able to manage psychological contracts and support an engaged workforce. This includes good HR data, integrated planning process, and future oriented competency management.

An employee engagement strategy requires a targeted communication and information strategy, employee participation, and managers who support the concepts of promoting employee motivation and engagement. Experience in various OECD countries has shown that such actions can provide a powerful counterbalance to the austerity-driven measures outlined in Chapter 2 of this report. A loss of trust, as well as continuing tense circumstances, can be minimised in the long term only through transparent communication on an institutional and individual level. Even more compelling may be the preventative impacts of a focus on engagement; since organisations will likely weather change and transition better if they start with a high level of engagement from their workforce.

Engagement has primarily positive connotations, but can also be understood in a negative sense if it appears that employees are being asked to improve their attitude and performance without receiving anything in return. The analysis in this report reinforces the notion that engagement is not only the responsibility of the individual employee, but also that of the employer, who is the driving force responsible for designing the right working conditions that lead to better engagement. This implies that engagement models should be embedded in a holistic HRM model with leadership and working conditions to foster engagement and measures to evaluate the effects and success. Engagement should be a factor of consideration in all HRM reforms, whether intended to cut size and costs or increase employer attractiveness.

Going forward: Identifying the underlying drivers of civil service capacity

Employee engagement surveys are not an end unto themselves; but provide a basis for objective management discussions, data to adjust policies, incentives for organisations to improve and a way to communicate the importance of the employee to meeting organisational objectives. By focusing on aligning objectives, engagement conversations can also help make more explicit the changing challenges and pressures faced by the public sector, and the role of both employee and organisations to respond. This helps build ownership for some of the difficult decisions that will have to be made, and supports more agile and tailored HRM measures.

Looking forward, the question is not how big or small should the workforce be, but what kind of employee is required to meet the challenges facing public administrations today and into the future. If CPAs are to become and remain leaner, countries cannot afford to have employees who are not ready to commit their full selves and skillsets to solving the complex challenges that define today's public sector work. In short, countries cannot afford to have unengaged employees. Countries need to invest in the conditions that create engagement to secure the future capacity of their workforce and, by extension, government.

OECD analysis on public workforce management will continue to support governments who seek to boost employee engagement and build a world class civil service. By leveraging the OECD's unique data on strategic HRM, and working through communities such as the Public Employment and Management working party and the Public Governance Committee, the OECD will contribute to the most pressing public workforce challenges and opportunities through, for example:

- Helping governments to make the most of employee surveys, including exploring the possibility of developing a survey module to enable international benchmarking. Enabling comparative benchmarking across OECD countries through employee surveys can support increased dialogue and awareness as countries seek to identify and develop drivers of civil service effectiveness.
- Developing insights on skills and competency requirements for high capacity civil services. As has been argued in this report, engagement can serve as a foundation for attracting people with the right skills, and can ensure that these people are supported to put their skills to the most effective use.
- Continued focus on public leadership and the management of senior managers. The OECD gathers unique data on the systems that support top leadership, including: development, appointments, performance and accountability, and the political administrative interface.
- Identifying opportunities to leverage diversity and inclusion in the public workforce for a more inclusive and tolerant society. A focus on engagement recognises that employees are individuals who have unique needs and talents, backgrounds, perspectives and identities. Ensuring that diversity in all its forms translates into workplace inclusion is a prerequisite to harness the creative and transformative potential that diversity brings to the civil service.
- Drive workforce productivity through better and more strategic people management. The cost of the public workforce is one of the most significant operational investments governments make. The OECD will continue to produce

evidence and analysis on how to optimise this investment to ensure that public resource get the best value from their workforce investments.

Results from the survey, discussed in Chapter 2, indicate that employee engagement across OECD countries may have been threatened as a result of the cost-cutting measures implemented in most OECD countries. Chapter 2 looks at these measures with a view to their potential longer-term impact on employees, organisations and the fiscal bottom line. Chapter 3 looks in more detail at the concept of engagement, how some countries are actively managing for engagement, and what kinds of leadership and HRM systems are required to address engagement in the CPAs of OECD countries.

References

Teague, P. and W.K. Roche (2014), "Recessionary bundles: HR practices in the Irish economic crisis", *Human Resource Management Journal*, Vol. 24, No 2, pp. 176-192.

Ulrich, D. (1997), *Human resource champions: The next agenda for adding value and delivering results*, Harvard Business School Press, Boston, MA.

MacLeod, D. Clarke N. (2009), *Engaging for Success: Enhancing performance through employee engagement*, BIS, London.

Chapter 2.

Budgetary constraints, cost cutting measures and civil service reform

This chapter looks at recent OECD research that suggests changes to human resource management (HRM) between 2008 and 2013 have been driven first and foremost by a reactive need to cut workforce costs, rather than building longer-term workforce capacity and innovation. It explores the survey results from the Survey on Managing Budgeting Constraints: Implications for HRM and Employment in Central Public Administration, which indicate that employee engagement across OECD countries may have been threatened as a result of the cost-cutting measures implemented in most OECD countries. Chapter 2 looks at these measures with a view to their potential longer-term impact on employees, organisations and the fiscal bottom line.

Introduction and overview

Central public administrations (CPAs) are undergoing processes of profound change in most OECD countries. While some of these changes can be associated with the 2008 economic and financial crisis, overall, pressures for change come from many sources. Important transformations are also being implemented in countries that have been less seriously impacted by the 2008 financial crisis, such as Switzerland, Finland and Sweden. Many of these changes also concern human resource management (HRM) policy areas not included in this survey, such as pensions, accountability and changes in the national social dialogue.

While pressures, priorities and objectives vary considerably, the data illustrate that budgetary constraints have a very strong impact on HRM systems. This does not only concern the (higher) number of implemented cost reduction measures, but also the quality of the measures that were implemented. In all cases, budgetary constraints have supported the view that the most important objectives of HRM measures are saving resources, increasing organisational performance and enhancing flexibility.

Despite the existing differences amongst the 32 examined countries, all national CPAs have shown a tremendous ability to react to changes. Public perceptions frequently suggest that CPAs are resistant to change and suffer from inertia. Instead, this survey will show that "long-standing taken for granted assumptions and orthodoxies no longer hold" (Ferlie et al., 2007).

Box 2.1. Budgetary constraints in OECD countries

The OECD has classified countries according to financial consolidation requirements in the 2012 update to *Restoring public finances* (OECD, 2012). Throughout this report, countries with high budgetary constraints are discussed and compared to countries with lower constraints. Given the time period considered in this report (2008-2013), countries with high budgetary constraints are generally understood to be those with particularly high consolidation requirements during that time, such as Greece, Ireland, Portugal, and Spain. Countries such as Germany, Sweden, Finland and Canada are considered to be among those with the lowest budgetary constraints. This report does not classify all countries according to fiscal consolidation requirements, but does give an indication of the differing levels of fiscal pressure faced by OECD countries.

Box 2.1. Budgetary constraints in OECD countries *(continued)*

Figure 2.1. Consolidation requirements to reduce government debt to 60% of GDP (2010-2013)

Change in underlying primary balance, percentage points of GDP

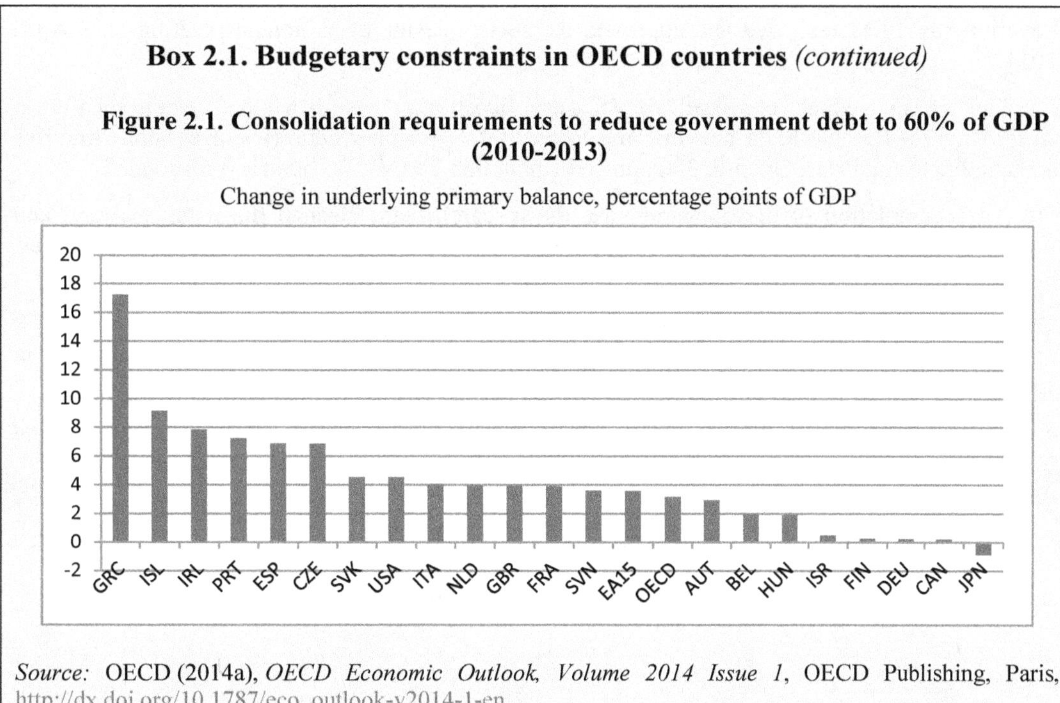

Source: OECD (2014a), *OECD Economic Outlook, Volume 2014 Issue 1*, OECD Publishing, Paris, http://dx.doi.org/10.1787/eco_outlook-v2014-1-en.

Budgetary constraints and HRM bundles

This survey collects data (see annex for methodology) regarding approximately 40 different HRM policies and instruments in 32 countries (28 of which are OECD member countries – see overview chart for breakdown Figure 2.2). These have been grouped into seven HRM bundles:

1. Public employment (e.g. downsizing)
2. Salary system
3. Training system
4. Cost-saving measures
5. Working hours and working time
6. Job security
7. Employment status (e.g. civil servants vs. public employees)

Box 2.2. Survey methodology

The survey, *Managing budgeting constraints: Implications for HRM and employment in central public administration*, that forms the basis of this first part of the report, aimed to assess the impact of budgetary constraints on HRM policies in national Central Public Administrations (CPA), between 2008 and 2013. The study explores trends and reform outcomes at the CPA level. The research is comparative and evidence-based, drawing on previous OECD surveys, existing academic studies,and literature reviews.

The survey was carried out in co-operation with the Working Party on Public Employment and Management (PEM), which is a network of top-officials from all OECD countries governments. PEM reviewed and approved the survey design at its annual meeting on 8 April 2014.

The survey, which consisted of 46 core questions, was distributed electronically in April/May 2014 to the PEM network and to all OECD member countries, accession countries and candidate countries. Overall, 32 countries (including 28 OECD countries) responded.

After completion of the questionnaire, the research team cleaned the data, analysed and filtered all answers, and identified those that were either still missing or unclear. In those cases, the respective countries were contacted.

In order to cross-check, validate and discuss the national answers and the survey, a discussion with representatives from all member states was held during the PEM meeting in spring 2015.

Source: OECD (2016), *HRM survey (Managing Budgeting Constraints Implications for HRM and Employment in Central Public Administration)*, OECD, Paris, http://qdd.oecd.org/subject.aspx?Subject=985A031D-9D64-4E13-B46F-2189F2447481.

Figure 2.2. Number of HRM measures implemented (2008-2013)

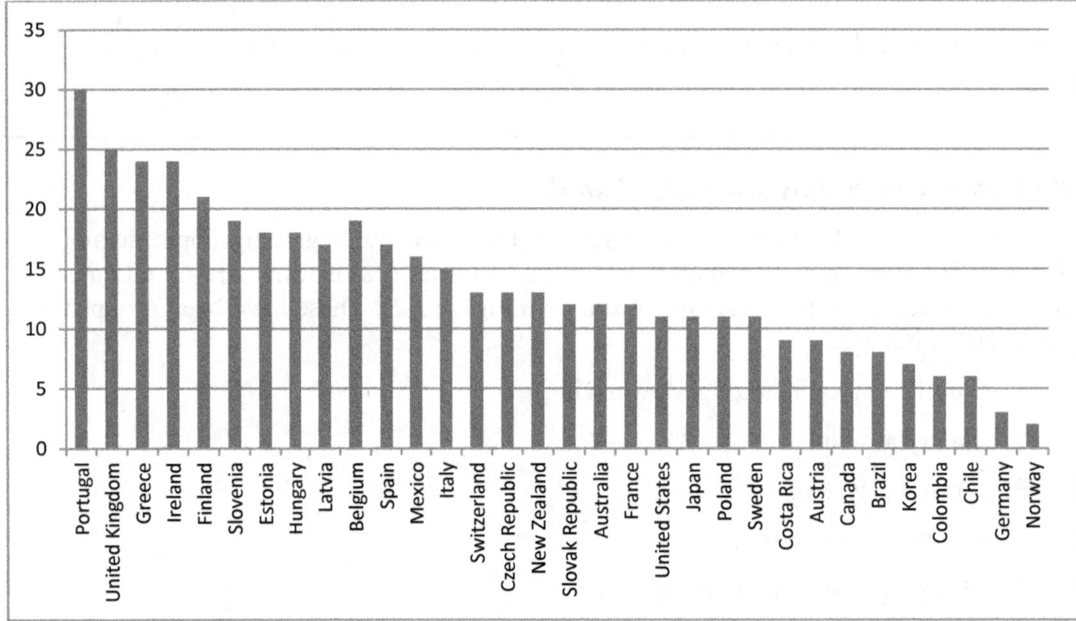

Source: OECD (2014b), *Survey on Managing Budgeting Constraints: Implications for HRM and Employment in Central Public Administration*, OECD, Paris, www.oecd.org/gov/pem/2014-human-resource-management-survey.pdf.

Figure 1.3 confirms a correlation between budgetary pressures and the number of measures implemented. Overall, the countries that have implemented the most measures addressed in the survey are also those with high budgetary pressures. Portugal, Greece, the United Kingdom and Ireland have implemented the highest number of such measures since 2008. The more budgetary pressures, the more measures are focused on cost-control. Countries such as Greece and Portugal have implemented almost all measures in this survey. Countries with the highest budgetary pressures are also implementing tougher downsizing measures (including the dismissal of public employees, cutting of salaries, freezing of promotion opportunities and cutting training budgets). On the other hand, countries with modest budgetary pressures, such as Germany, Norway, Sweden and Japan, have implemented fewer and softer measures.

There are a number of exceptions. The Czech Republic has implemented a relatively low number of measures despite, arguably, high budgetary pressure. Belgium has implemented the highest number of measures in the "employment status" HR bundle.

Finland and Switzerland have implemented a high number of cost reduction measures, despite relatively low budgetary pressure, which can be explained by the fact that other factors (such as political considerations) play an important role in the reform process. Budgetary pressures are, therefore, an important, but not exclusive, trigger for reforms and cost reduction. Pollitt and Bouckaert (2011) discuss the important role of administrative elites and political interests in the reform process. In some cases, other international, national and sector contexts, and the social dialogue, also play an important role.

Restructuring and downsizing central public administration

Figure 2.3. Changes in central public administration employment levels (2008-2013)

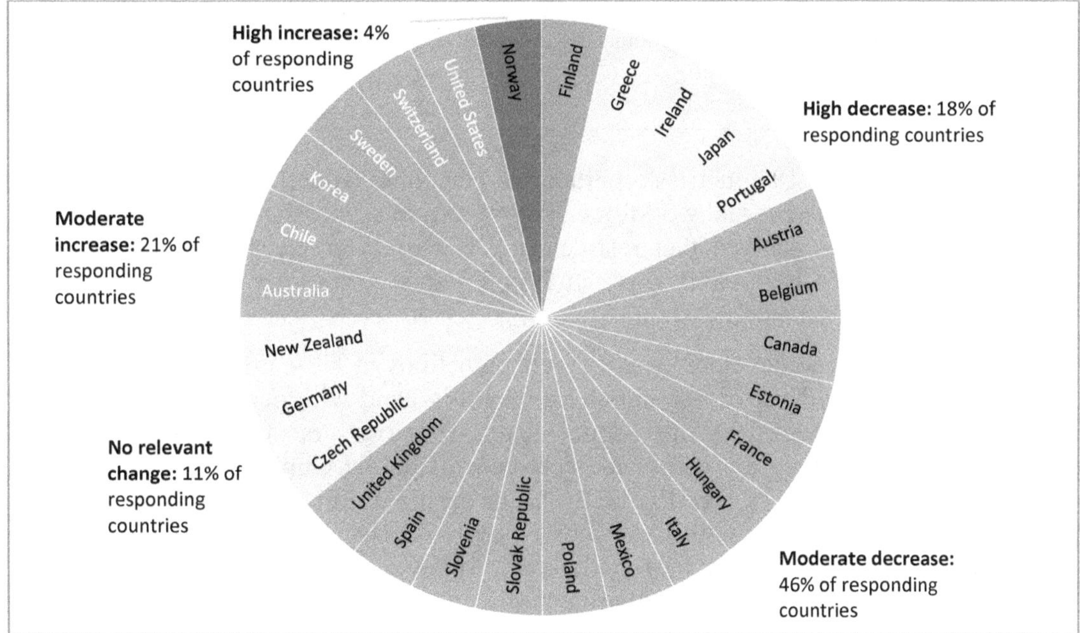

Source: OECD (2014b), Question 1, *Survey on Managing Budgeting Constraints: Implications for HRM and Employment in Central Public Administration*, OECD, Paris, www.oecd.org/gov/pem/2014-human-resource-management-survey.pdf.

From 2008-2013, downsizing trends took place in most OECD countries' CPAs. This was one of the most important employment trends in the CPAs of OECD countries, however, the details reveal large differences regarding employment developments in different sectors (and organisations), the choice of instruments and the importance of measures.

Almost all European Union (EU) countries reported a process of employment reduction in their CPAs between 2008 and 2013. Only Sweden increased CPA employment. Germany and the Czech Republic stabilised CPA employment (in the case of Germany after many years of reductions).

Box 2.3. Employment reductions in select OECD countries' central public administrations

Belgium: reductions were -7.05% over a period of eight years (2006-2013), although there was an acceleration in more recent years (in comparison to 2006): -7.05% (2013); -5.26% (2012); -2.83% (2011). This diminution in the workforce is due to two factors: 1) strategic workforce planning based on a selective substitution policy; and 2) the ageing of staff. It is difficult to separate those two factors, as of the 4 591 staff to have supposedly left the federal civil service in 2011, 2 257 (49%) retired.

Greece has decreased employment in its CPA by 19% since 2010. By December 2015, Greece was obliged to reduce public employment (of general government) by at least 150 000 compared to 2010.

Ireland reduced public service staffing levels by 10% between 2008 and the first quarter (Q1) of 2014.

Portugal reduced CPA employment by 8.9% between 31 December 2011 and March 2014.

Source: OECD (2014b), Survey on Managing Budgeting Constraints: Implications for HRM and Employment in Central Public Administration, OECD, Paris, http://www.oecd.org/gov/pem/2014-human-resource-management-survey.pdf.

During the survey, 18 countries reported that personnel reductions are taking place in order to restructure the internal workforce. This is also in accordance with other statistics in this survey, which showed that restructuring is closely connected with downsizing strategies, and, as the Belgian example in Box 2.3 shows, can often allow states to do more logical and informed downsizing.

Regarding sectorial developments, overall reductions in CPA employment focus on the central ministries/departments and can go hand-in-hand with occasional increases in other agencies or sectors at the central level. However, most countries reporting reductions state that they are across the spectrum of public employment at the central level explored in the survey (see Figure 2.3). For example, Ireland, Portugal and Greece report high decreases across the four sectors analysed (in Greece central government agencies were only moderately impacted). Italy, Spain, and the United Kingdom report the same level of reductions across all groups.

France, Poland and Japan report employment increases in central government agencies while reducing employment in ministries, which suggests a reallocation of resources from policy functions towards service delivery. Only countries that report increases in employment overall also report increases in health and education employment at the central level. The one exception is Austria, which reports reductions in all areas except a moderate increase in education. In Estonia and Finland, reductions seem to have been concentrated in ministries and agencies, with employment in education and health services left stable. Countries with lower budgetary constraints appear able to be more selective and strategic regarding sector employment levels, whereas countries with higher budgetary constraints seek reductions at all levels.

Figure 2.4. Central public administration employment reductions by policy sector (percent of responding countries) (2008-2013)

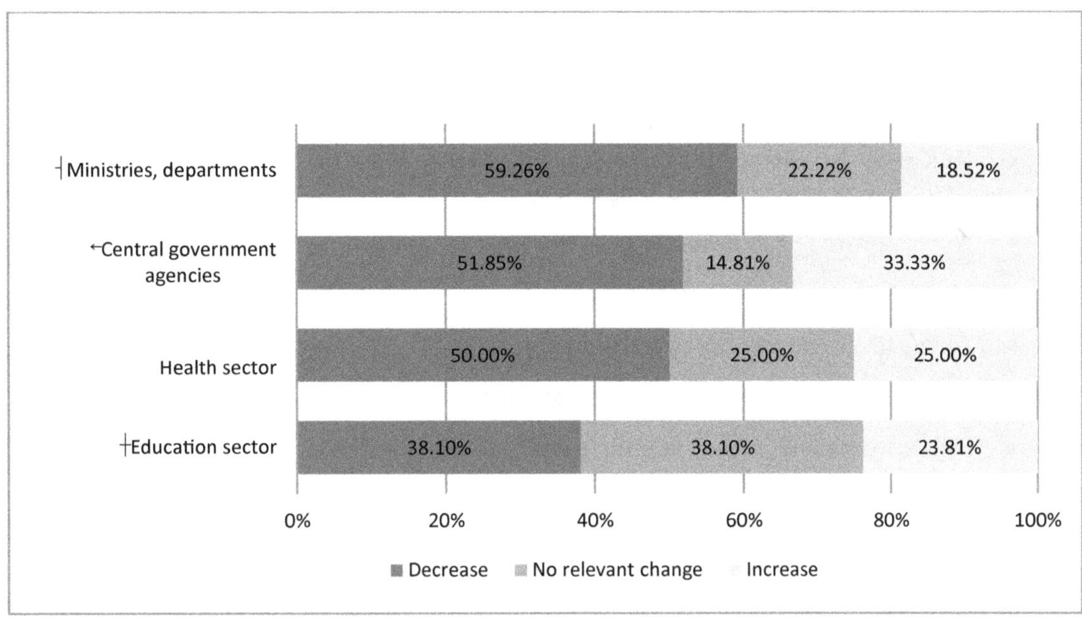

Source: OECD (2014b), Question 2, *Survey on Managing Budgeting Constraints: Implications for HRM and Employment in Central Public Administration*, OECD, Paris, www.oecd.org/gov/pem/2014-human-resource-management-survey.pdf.

Overall, OECD countries have reduced employment more at the central ministerial level than in the education and health sectors. This is because downsizing is more difficult in sectors and policy fields that have become more important in recent years, or that have mandatory service levels. Education is often seen as an investment in future growth, and the health sector is becoming more important in the context of demographic changes. Health expenditures are also often non-discretionary; countries are obliged to deliver them. On the other hand, some countries are in the process of shifting employment on the ministerial level to central government agencies.

The fact that downsizing takes place almost everywhere illustrates that some countries reduce public employment as a result of factors that do not correspond to budgetary constraints, for example, the need to meet demographic challenges, or as a result of restructuring measures and governance reforms to improve effectiveness, such as the decentralisation of public employment or the modernisation of work systems.

Box 2.4. Responsible restructuring

The term responsible restructuring was coined by Cascio (2002/2005). Cascio differentiates between companies that see employees either as costs or as assets to be developed. He concludes that often, the pure cost restructuring approach produces ten mistakes:

- Failure to be clear about long- and short-term goals and the failure to consider alternative approaches to reducing costs.
- Use of downsizing as a first resort, rather than as a last resort.
- Use of non-selective downsizing.
- Failure to change the ways work is done.
- Failure to involve workers in the restructuring process.
- Failure to communicate openly and honestly.
- Inept handling of those who lose their jobs.
- Failure to manage survivors effectively.
- Ignoring the effects on other stakeholders.
- Failure to evaluate the results of downsizing policies.

Consequently, Cascio advocates responsible restructuring as an alternative to pure restructuring/downsizing. According to Cascio, responsible restructuring includes:

- "Carefully consider the rationale behind restructuring. Invest in analysis and consider the impact on those who stay, those who leave, and the ability of the organisation to serve its customers" (Cascio, 2005: 48).
- Consider the virtues of stability.
- Before making decisions, managers should make their concerns known to the workforce.
- Do not use downsizing as a "quick-fix" to achieve short-term goals.
- If dismissals are carried out, the process should be as fair as possible and be explained in a consistent manner.
- Regular communication is vital in the process.
- "Give survivors a reason to stay, and prospective new hires a reason to join" (Cascio, 2005: 48).
- Continue to train employees and managers in the new context.
- Examine all HRM policies in light of the changes taking place.

Source: Cascio, W. (2005), "Strategies for Responsible Restructuring", in *Academy of Management Executive*, 2005, Vol. 19, No. 4.

The use of instruments to restructure and reduce employment

Figure 2.5. Instruments used to restructure and reduce employment in Central Public Administrations (2008-2013)

	#Countries	Australia	Austria	Belgium	Canada	Chile	Czech Rep	Estonia	Finland	France	Germany	Greece	Hungary	Ireland	Italy	Japan	Korea	Mexico	New Zealand	Norway	Poland	Portugal	Slovak Rep	Slovenia	Spain	Sweden	Switzerland	United Kingdom	United States	Colombia	Latvia	Costa Rica	Brazil
Employment Measures																																	
Privatisation	9			●			●		●							●	●		●							●		●					●
Decentralisation of employment	9			●			●	●	●	●								●			●											●	●
Supporting voluntary departures	13					●			●	●		●	●	●	●	●		●	●			●						●	●				
Dismissals	18	●			●	●	●	●	●			●	●					●			●	●	●	●	●	●	●	●			●		
Annual productivity targets	19	●	●	●			●		●	●		●	●	●			●	●	●			●	●	●		●	●	●			●		
Outsourcing	23		●	●		●	●		●	●		●		●	●	●	●	●	●		●	●			●	●		●	●	●	●	●	●
Recruitment freeze	28	●		●	●		●	●	●	●		●	●	●	●	●	●	●	●		●	●	●	●	●	●	●	●	●	●	●	●	●
Non or partial replacement of retiring persons	28	●	●	●	●	●	●		●	●		●	●	●	●	●		●	●		●	●	●	●	●	●	●	●	●	●	●	●	●
Numbers of Measures		4	3	6	3	4	7	3	8	6	0	6	5	5	4	5	4	7	6	0	5	6	4	4	4	6	4	7	4	3	5	4	5

Source: OECD (2014b), Question 5, *Survey on Managing Budgeting Constraints: Implications for HRM and Employment in Central Public Administration*, OECD, Paris, www.oecd.org/gov/pem/2014-human-resource-management-survey.pdf.

National responses show significant differences amongst countries with high budgetary pressures and low budgetary pressures. Countries with the highest budgetary pressures have been active in using all downsizing instruments included in the survey. In most cases, they have not replaced retiring staff, have set annual productivity targets, and have applied recruitment freezes. Portugal, Latvia, the Slovak Republic and the Czech Republic report frequent dismissals of public employees. Countries with lower budgetary pressures have also been active in different ways, however, they focus less on instruments such as the decentralisation and shifting of employment, privatisation and outsourcing, and more on the non- or partial-replacement of retiring staff.

Figure 2.6. Use of downsizing instruments (percent of responding countries) (2008-2013)

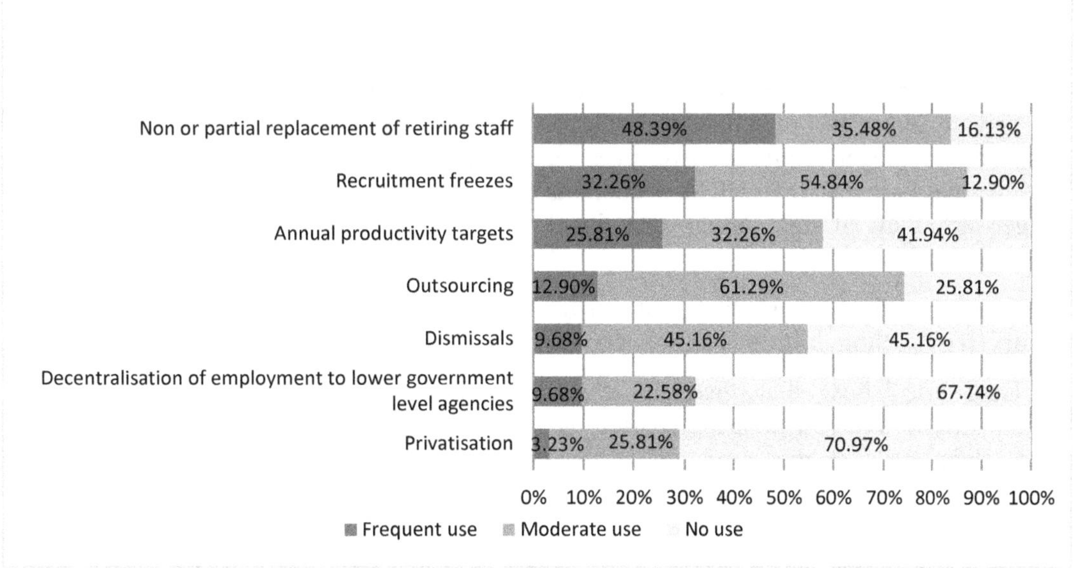

Source: OECD (2014b), Question 5, *Survey on Managing Budgeting Constraints: Implications for HRM and Employment in Central Public Administration*, OECD, Paris, www.oecd.org/gov/pem/2014-human-resource-management-survey.pdf.

Downsizing can be related to restructuring policies and strategic management issues. In order to gain more knowledge on the link between downsizing and strategic management, countries were asked the following question: "If personnel reductions are taking place, to which of the following strategic objectives are they related?"

Figure 2.7. Relation between personnel reductions and strategic objectives (number of countries) (2008 -2013)

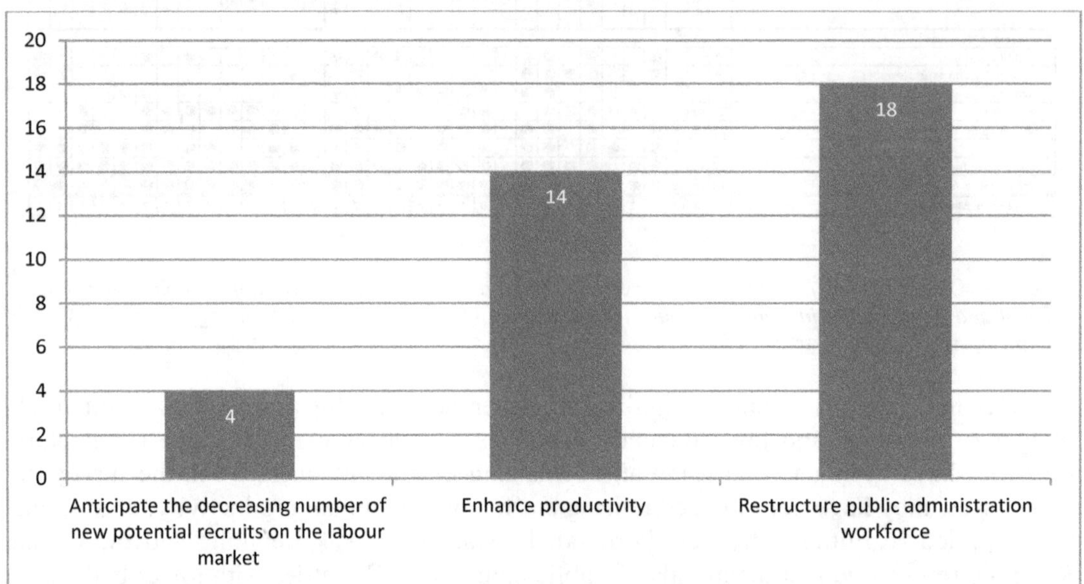

Source: OECD (2014b), Question 6b, *Survey on Managing Budgeting Constraints: Implications for HRM and Employment in Central Public Administration*, OECD, Paris, www.oecd.org/gov/pem/2014-human-resource-management-survey.pdf.

Overall, only four countries (Finland, Belgium, Sweden, and Mexico) responded that downsizing is carried out in order to anticipate the decreasing number of new potential recruits in the labour market. This is a surprisingly low number, as many countries with very high demographic pressures find themselves in a tough competitive situation with the private sector in order to attract talented people from a smaller pool of candidates. This may have been temporarily relieved during the economic downturn, but the survey's finding may suggest that HRM reductions are not being primarily undertaken with a longer-term view of civil service capacity. This is discussed in greater detail in Chapter 3 this report.

Fourteen countries replied that downsizing is linked with strategies to increase productivity, although little is known about how the two issues are linked in practice.

Data also show that there is a strong relationship between restructuring and downsizing: often, restructuring is used as a synonym for downsizing the workforce. In more than 40% of the surveyed countries, restructuring measures were sometimes combined with workforce dismissals.

Although the way "restructuring" is implemented is likely to be highly context-specific, and therefore will differ across OECD countries, the survey indicates a number of ways restructuring takes place, with the most important distinction being between external and internal restructuring.

With external restructuring, a majority of countries report some use of outsourcing between 2008-2013, as a means of reducing public employment, with fewer reporting decentralisation of employment to lower levels of government and privatisation measures. Outsourcing, decentralising or, simply, shifting personnel to other administrative bodies, may only disguise changes in workforce structure and developments towards the "shadow state", which means "that many workers providing public services financed by the government are actually employed by the private or third sector" (Bach and Kessler, 2012). Almost all countries with the highest budgetary pressures are trying to reduce CPA employment levels by outsourcing public services.

For internal restructuring, eight countries reported that they had reduced/cut hierarchical levels or careers in CPAs. This can be seen as a way to reform bureaucracies, flatten hierarchies and cut red tape. From an HRM development point of view, it is important to note that cutting hierarchical levels and careers often has a significant impact on career development opportunities and promotions. Six countries reported that promotion opportunities were frozen/put on hold.

Recruitment freeze

Between 2008 and 2013, almost all countries implemented recruitment freeze measures. Ten OECD countries replied that they are "frequently" using this instrument; fourteen countries answered that they use this instrument to a "moderate degree". Countries with very high budgetary pressures either use this instrument "frequently" or to a "moderate" degree. Three countries with modest budgetary pressures reported not using this instrument at all. The OECD has shown that recruitment freezes can, "create problems with the structure, allocation and skills base that can take a long time to repair" (OECD, 2011), and tend to draw out the reduction process, which can have prolonged negative impacts on staff motivation and morale. The apparently widespread use of this instrument raises questions for the longer-term capacity and renewal of civil services, especially in a context of ageing public workforces.

Voluntary termination and employee turnover

Many organisations use voluntary turnover to reduce public employment levels and control costs. Voluntary termination may also include buy-out offers as another way of downsizing a workforce. A challenge here is in determining who leaves and who stays, in order to avoid losing high performers and particular essential skillsets.

Thirteen responding countries indicated that measures have been introduced to encourage voluntary departures. These are split between measures to encourage early retirement (nine countries), and/or leaving allowances (eight countries), which are often a part of voluntary exit schemes.

The results of these questions illustrate that there appears to be very little ability to track the effects of these policies. Figure 2.8 shows that just under half of respondents indicated that they are unable to say whether these policies have been successful at encouraging staff to leave. Even more striking, the vast majority of countries who have implemented such measures have been unable to say whether they have resulted in any efficiency gains.

Figure 2.8. Reported effects of voluntary departure programmes (number of countries) (2008-2013)

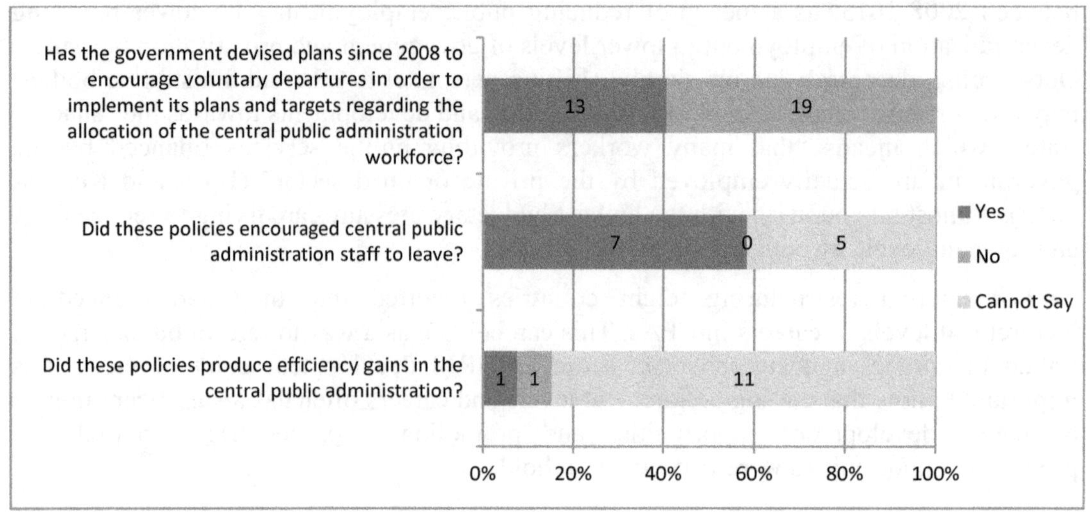

Source: OECD (2014b), Questions 15, 15c and 15d, *Survey on Managing Budgeting Constraints: Implications for HRM and Employment in Central Public Administration*, OECD, Paris, www.oecd.org/gov/pem/2014-human-resource-management-survey.pdf.

Two countries report the use of "dismissals" frequently, and fourteen countries to a "moderate" degree. These numbers show that half of all analysed countries have dismissed employees due to budgetary constraints, demonstrating that "job security" has become a relative concept in the public sector. Whereas in the past it was possible to dismiss central public employees because of misbehaviour, 14 countries reported that measures have been implemented to allow the dismissal of the CPA workforce for reasons other than misbehaviour, illegal conduct and poor performance.

Figure 2.9. Frequency of dismissals (percent of responding countries) (2008-2013)

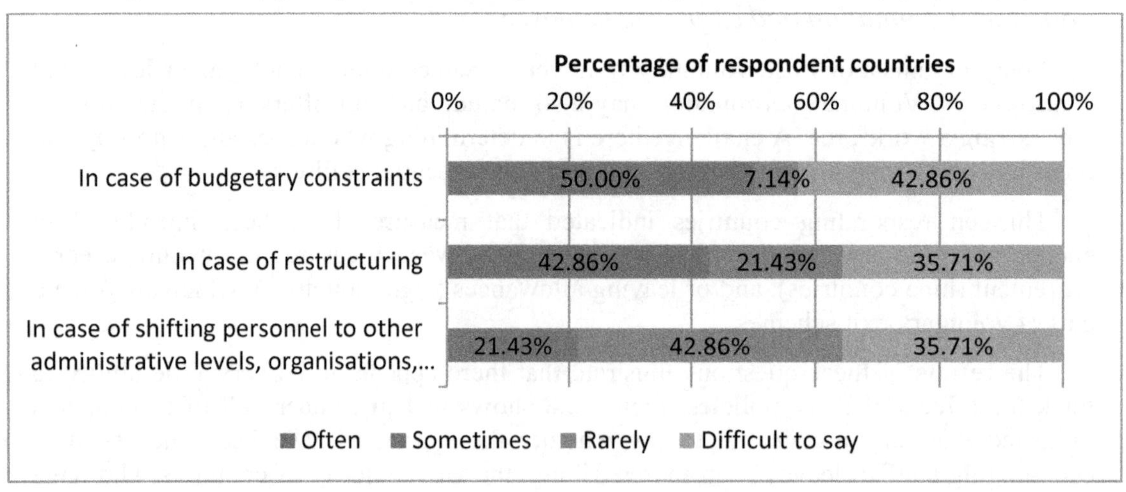

Source: OECD (2014b), Question 14b, *Survey on Managing Budgeting Constraints: Implications for HRM and Employment in Central Public Administration*, OECD, Paris, www.oecd.org/gov/pem/2014-human-resource-management-survey.pdf.

There is no clear link between the degree of budgetary pressures and compulsory termination. For example, Ireland did not refer to compulsory termination, whereas Sweden applied this instrument to a moderate degree. Thus, the use of compulsory termination seems to be linked to other contextual variables, such as the national social dialogue, status issues and the degree of job protection. For example, in Sweden, civil servants can be dismissed, but still enjoy a high degree of job protection.

Civil service job security after 2008

Writers on public administration have long suggested that without a specific status, legal protection, lifetime tenure and special ethical rules, our societies would be open to terrible corruption (*furchtbarer Korruption* – Weber), which would undermine the capacity of the state to rule society. In most countries, job security in the public sector is both an important motivational element for the recruitment and the retention of staff, and a way to provide independence and protection from undesired forms of politicisation. At present, most countries still agree with the argument that job security is important, but many suggest that the highest levels of job security can only be justified for specific positions and functions.

Lifetime employment appears to be less prominent than it was some decades ago, with many countries moving away from the classical lifetime tenure principle. In more countries it is now possible to dismiss civil servants for various reasons (mostly cases of poor performance). Countries with a more traditional bureaucratic career system still have a higher degree of job security. Thus, if a country decides to reform its traditional career structure, it is also likely that it will reconsider traditional job security patterns. For example Portugal, which has completely reformed traditional bureaucratic employment features.

Current downsizing trends in many countries show that it would be misleading to speak generally about the "stability of public service employment". In fact, people often have a false image of employment in the public sector as they believe that it is more stable than employment in the private sector. Austria, Colombia, Latvia, the United Kingdom, Portugal, Poland, Spain and Austria reported that there were more personnel cuts in the CPA than in the private sector.

The trend towards the relaxation of job security is not also a trend towards a continuous weakening of job protection for civil servants. Overall, (only) five countries reported that it has become easier to dismiss public employees, and (only) four countries have also eased job protection for civil servants. Thus, despite the trend towards less job security, many countries seem to maintain a high degree of job security for central administration employees.

Figure 2.10. Changes to the employment protection of public employees and civil servants (percent of responding countries) (2008-2013)

	Yes	No	Cannot say
It has become easier to dismiss public employees	17.86%	75.00%	7.14%
It has become easier to dismiss civil servants	14.29%	82.14%	3.57%
Notice periods have been shortened	7.14%	85.71%	7.14%

Source: OECD (2014b), Question 18, *Survey on Managing Budgeting Constraints: Implications for HRM and Employment in Central Public Administration*, OECD, Paris, www.oecd.org/gov/pem/2014-human-resource-management-survey.pdf.

The degree of job security in the CPA is still high, but "relative" and closely connected to the national context, status and the national social dialogue etc. However, budgetary pressures, combined with a country's desire to establish more workforce agility, mobility, innovation and exchange with private and third sectors, may also be a justification for reconsidering the job security levels of some categories of employees, and for looking at alternative contract regimes for specific professions.

Compensation in the civil service: Freezes and reductions

Figure 2.11. Reductions to compensation (2008-2013)

	#Countries	Australia	Austria	Belgium	Canada	Chile	Czech Rep	Estonia	Finland	France	Germany	Greece	Hungary	Ireland	Italy	Japan	Korea	Mexico	New Zealand	Norway	Poland	Portugal	Slovak Rep	Slovenia	Spain	Sweden	Switzerland	United Kingdom	United States	Colombia	Latvia	Costa Rica	Brazil
Remuneration System Measures																																	
Reduction of remuneration for top-level	6											●	●	●	●			●															●
Reduction of remuneration for all staff	6											●		●								●		●	●						●		
Reduction or abolishment of allowances	10				●			●				●	●	●								●	●	●	●						●		
Reduction of Performance Related Pay	9							●					●	●	●						●	●		●				●			●		
Pay freeze	15						●	●		●		●	●	●	●		●	●			●	●	●	●	●			●					
Other	11	●		●			●				●					●			●					●		●		●		●		●	
Numbers of Measures		1	0	1	1	0	2	3	0	1	1	4	4	5	3	1	1	2	1	0	2	4	2	5	3	1	0	3	0	1	3	1	1

Source: OECD (2014b), Question 7c, Survey on Managing Budgeting Constraints: Implications for HRM and Employment in Central Public Administration, OECD, Paris, www.oecd.org/gov/pem/2014-human-resource-management-survey.pdf.

Compensation is arguably one of the most critical influences on the quality and effectiveness of human resources. Along with values and workplace quality, compensation has a direct relationship with attraction and retention. Compensation is one of various factors that excerpt influence on motivation and performance, fairness perceptions and the quality of the work. Compensation levels directly drive the overall cost of public sector employment. In virtually every aspect of organisational functioning, compensation can shape employee behaviour and organisational effectiveness (Gupta and Shaw, 2014).

Compensation systems in OECD countries have been subject to significant cuts. Between 2008 and 2013, almost 75% of all responding countries (around 70% of which are EU member states) introduced changes to their remuneration systems to reduce costs.

Box 2.5. Cuts to civil servant compensation in select OECD countries

Portugal implemented wage cuts, suspensions of performance bonuses and decreases of overtime pay.

Spain implemented a salary cut in 2010, and in 2012, the extra December payment was not paid to civil servants. In 2015, 25% of this bonus was paid.

Poland froze pay in the civil service in 2009. It was decided to extend this freeze until 2016. In 2009, the scale that determines the basic pay of civil service corps members and the civil service bonus (paid to the civil servants only) was changed. A special bonus of optional components of pay was also eliminated.

Hungary eliminated the 13th salary (13th month of wages paid each year).

Estonia abolished career-based salary components, such as additional remuneration for tenure, foreign languages, and academic degrees.

Belgium slowed down automatic pay increases by spreading the increases over more time, and by slowing down advancement if there is unsatisfactory performance.

Germany no longer takes seniority into account in middle and top management. For the remuneration of agents in professional and secretarial positions and technical support, pay regularly increases in eight levels in line with experience. Remuneration is also based on performance: agents effecting extraordinary performance can enter new levels faster; agents with low performance may not reach a new level in the regular periodic interval.

The Czech Republic increased the average salaries for top-level staff due to non-systematic changes introduced in 2011. The overall budget for state employees' remuneration decreased by 10%. This resulted in a decrease of salaries for a vast number of regular staff, and an increase in salaries for some managers.

Source: OECD (2014b), *Survey on Managing Budgeting Constraints: Implications for HRM and Employment in Central Public Administration*, OECD, Paris, www.oecd.org/gov/pem/2014-human-resource-management-survey.pdf.

Figure 2.12. Instruments for cutting civil servant compensation (percent of responding countries) (2008-2013)

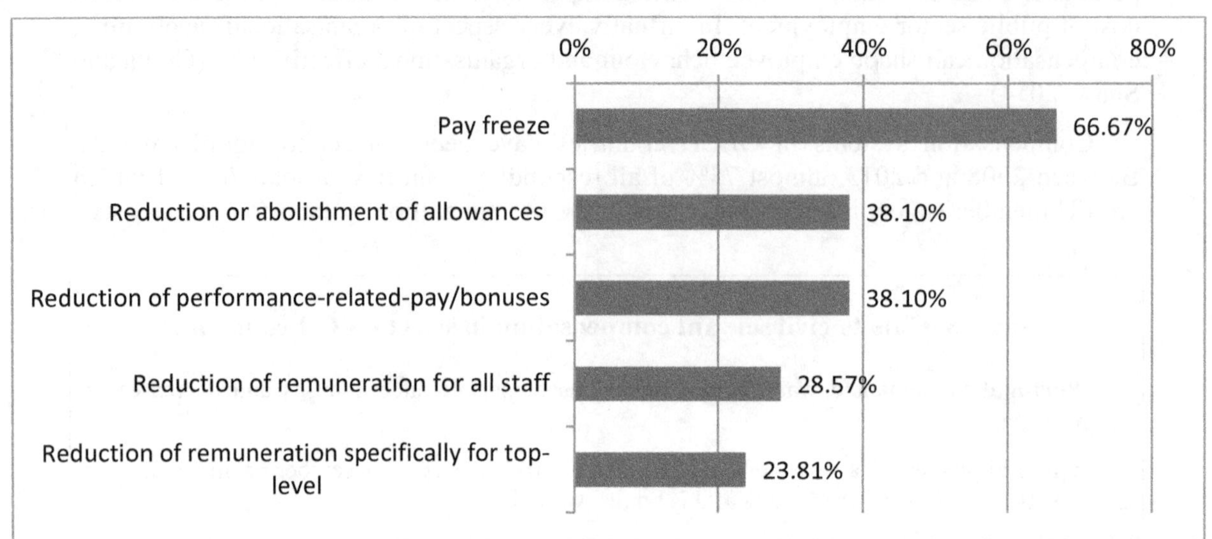

Source: OECD (2014b), Question 7c, *Survey on Managing Budgeting Constraints: Implications for HRM and Employment in Central Public Administration*, OECD, Paris, www.oecd.org/gov/pem/2014-human-resource-management-survey.pdf.

Fourteen OECD countries have implemented measures to freeze remuneration (sometimes for certain categories of staff); six countries cut remuneration levels for all categories of staff; and nine countries (particularly those with high budgetary pressures) reduced allowances, bonuses and performance related pay. Some countries with modest budgetary pressures did not implement any pay cuts. Chile, Norway, Sweden, Australia, Switzerland, Austria, Belgium, New Zealand, Germany and the United States did not cut remuneration levels. However, frozen pay levels with no cost of living increases result in the erosion of real wages. Overall, 67% of countries surveyed have implemented a pay freeze since 2008.

Performance related pay during the economic crisis

The main argument for performance related pay (PRP) is that it acts as a motivator by providing extrinsic rewards in the form of pay, and intrinsic rewards through the recognition of effort and achievement. PRP is also seen as helping employees to closely identify with the goals of the organisation, which leads to increased productivity, quality, flexibility and teamwork. In addition, PRP is seen to be useful in the recruitment and retention of staff.

Over the past 50 years, however, many researchers have questioned whether PRP actually acts as a motivator, or, indeed, if money can motivate. Empirical evidence in the United States, Australia and Malaysia questions whether PRP has enhanced individual performance (Taylor and Beh, 2013; Kellough and Nigro, 2002; Perry et al, 2009). Demmke (2009) suggests that modern PRP schemes are not necessarily fairer than traditional seniority pay. Whereas in the traditional system, the principle of seniority (everybody receives salary increases independently of his or her performance) may be at the centre of the "unfairness" debate; in systems with PRP and individual pay setting, the problem is that pay is linked to the discretion of managers (and the subjective allocation of PRP to those people who are supposed to perform better) and the perception of employees' (different) pay to that of their colleagues.

Data from this survey suggest that performance-related pay may be declining. Nine countries have reduced bonuses, allowances and performance related pay. However, Greece introduced a performance related pay system in 2014.

Overall, current trends in the field of pay are complex and contradictory. Whereas pay disparity and pay flexibility are increasing, feelings of being treated unfairly may be rising if performance related pay is not implemented properly. At the same time, there is still wide support for decentralised and flexible pay systems, and the need to align public and private pay settings (especially for top managers).

Training for civil servants: cuts and efficiency measures

Figure 2.13 Training system measures and reforms implemented (2008-2013)

	#Countries	Australia	Austria	Belgium	Canada	Chile	Czech Rep	Estonia	Finland	France	Germany	Greece	Hungary	Ireland	Italy	Japan	Korea	Mexico	New Zealand	Norway	Poland	Portugal	Slovak Rep	Slovenia	Spain	Sweden	Switzerland	United Kingdom	United States	Colombia	Latvia	Costa Rica	Brazil
Training System Measures																																	
Reduction of training days	10		●	●				●	●				●	●								●		●	●			●					
Reduce travel costs to travel to events	11	●	●		●			●	●			●		●				●				●							●		●		
Assessment of training needs	14	●		●								●	●	●				●			●	●	●				●	●	●	●	●		
Reduction of budgets	18		●	●			●	●	●					●	●			●			●	●	●	●	●		●	●	●		●		●
Shift employee training to employment desk	22	●	●	●	●			●	●			●	●				●	●		●	●	●	●	●	●		●	●	●	●		●	●
Have training policies been affected?	22	●	●	●			●	●	●			b	●	●	●			●			●	●	●	●	●	●	●	●	●		●	●	●
Measures introduced to increase efficiency?	24	●	●	●	●			●	●	●		●	●	●			●	●		●	●	●	●	●	●		●	●	●	●	●	●	
Numbers of Measures		5	6	6	3	0	2	6	6	1	0	4	5	6	2	0	2	6	0	2	5	7	5	5	5	1	5	6	6	3	5	3	3

Source: OECD (2014b), Question 9, *Survey on Managing Budgeting Constraints: Implications for HRM and Employment in Central Public Administration*, OECD, Paris, www.oecd.org/gov/pem/2014-human-resource-management-survey.pdf.

Training is increasingly discussed in the context of lifelong learning, knowledge management and skill development. Consequently, the importance of learning and training in a modern civil service should be growing, to ensure that civil servants are able to continually update their skills and innovate in response to fast changing political priorities, technological advances and citizen expectations. Metsma (2014) says that: "Training has many roles in central public administrations. Firstly, it is related to the implementation of tasks and focuses on developing skills and competencies in order to fulfil objectives of the organisation. Secondly, it is part of the motivation system and functions as an instrument to retain a high-quality and high performing workforce. And thirdly, training is an instrument to raise civil servants' awareness of their role and responsibility and introduce shared values among civil service staff". Bossaert et al (2008) also claim that training is linked to organisational performance and, as such, is an asset and an investment in human resources. Learning opportunities are often ranked as the most attractive features of jobs by recent graduates.

Despite the clear benefits of learning to public administrations, training budgets in OECD CPAs seem to be among the first items cut when fiscal stress hits. This has further implications for training programmes and training methods, as shrinking training budgets force organisations to prioritise training topics and seek more cost effective ways of delivering training (Metsma, 2014). However, training is one of many vehicles to develop skills, and therefore spending on training is an imperfect indicator of skills acquisition.

Overall, 22 countries reported that training policies have been affected by the financial crisis; 19 have implemented measures to raise the efficiency of training; 16 have reduced training budgets; and 10 have reduced the number of training days. The fact that Greece has not implemented measures is because most of their training budgets come from the European Social Funds, and are therefore not subject to the same austerity measures.

Figure 2.14. Reductions to civil servant training (percent of responding countries) (2008-2013)

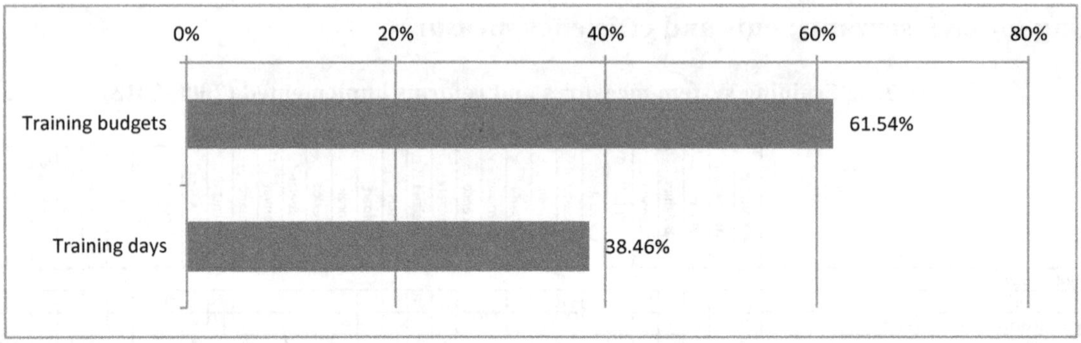

	Percent of responding countries
Training budgets	61.54%
Training days	38.46%

Source: OECD (2014b), Question 9b, *Survey on Managing Budgeting Constraints: Implications for HRM and Employment in Central Public Administration*, OECD, Paris, www.oecd.org/gov/pem/2014-human-resource-management-survey.pdf.

Only in Sweden, France, Germany, Norway, Chile, Canada, Korea and Columbia, were training policies unaffected by the financial crisis. Most countries with high budgetary constraints have implemented cuts to training.

There are significant differences amongst countries regarding the choice of measures in the field of training. OECD countries reported that they are introducing measures to make training more cost-effective by reducing travel costs to training events (in 11 countries), by centralising and streamlining training curricula (United Kingdom), by using training needs assessments to ensure that training is only provided when necessary (in 14 countries), and by shifting employee training to be readily available at employees' desks (computer-assisted e-training) (in 21 countries).

Figure 2.15. Measures introduced to raise the efficiency of civil servant training (percent of responding countries) (2008-2013)

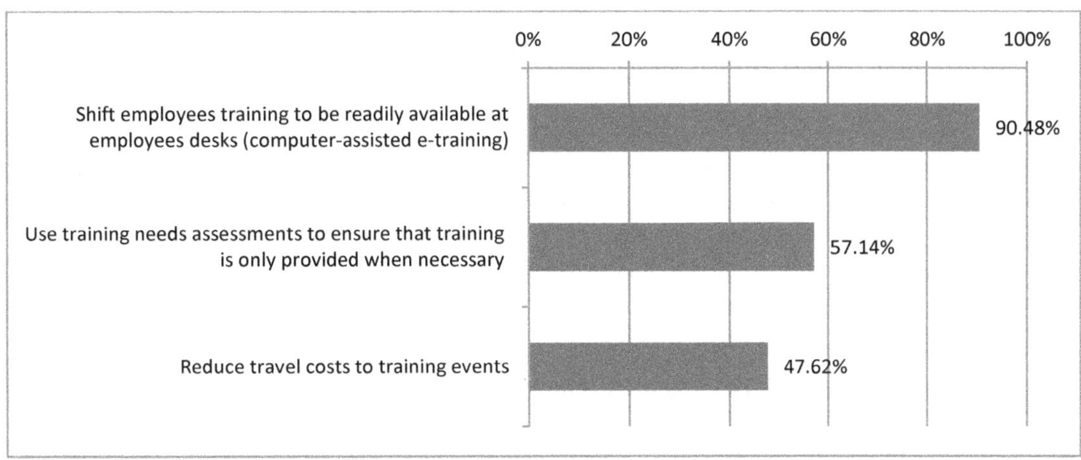

Source: OECD (2014b), Question 9e, *Survey on Managing Budgeting Constraints: Implications for HRM and Employment in Central Public Administration*, OECD, Paris, www.oecd.org/gov/pem/2014-human-resource-management-survey.pdf.

It is often difficult to separate cost cutting measures from efficiency measures. For example, in almost all OECD countries, in-house training has become more widespread, and outside-training activities have been reduced. Other reforms concern the creation of synergies to save resources, for example, the United Kingdom has created a single training curriculum to change what people learn and what is on offer. Since 2010, the Australian Public Service (APS) has adopted a strategy-driven approach to prioritise its investment in learning and development for skills and capabilities that are shared across the service (leadership development, talent development, core skills and management skills). The APS has also adopted a collective approach to designing and developing learning programmes for shared learning needs. This approach was not the result of pressures from the 2008 financial crisis, but was driven by an internal APS agenda to ensure that APS has the capability required to continue meeting the needs of citizens, and by the recognition that there was an opportunity to improve the efficiency and effectiveness of its collective investment in employee learning and development.

Overall, the trends toward cuts to training appear contradictory in times when employers and employees are calling for the need to invest in skill and competency development as part of national competition strategies. Reducing training budgets may have negative effects on the individual, organisation and the level of the CPA.

Unfortunately, the survey's data sample is too small to give a full picture of the situation. However, it indicates that there are reasons to believe that many countries focus on cutting costs rather than on implementing a wider and more sophisticated menu of measures and instruments that may reduce costs and raise the effectiveness of training (Stewart and Brown, 2011).

Effects on civil services and servants: Trust, stress, and opportunity

The situation in many OECD countries reflects what Levine illustrated thirty years ago: "We are entering a new era of public budgeting, personnel, and programme management. It is an era dominated by resource scarcity. It will be a period of hard times for government managers that will require them to manage cut-backs, tradeoffs, reallocations, organisational contractions, programme terminations, sacrifice, and the unfreezing and freeing up of grants and privileges that have come to be regarded as unnegotiable rights, entitlements, and contracts. It will be a period desperately in need of the development of a methodology for what I call 'cutback management'" (Levine, 1979: 179).

So far, there is not enough empirical evidence that suggests the measures described above have been effective, or not, in achieving the intended benefits. Generally, the literature distinguishes between the financial, organisational, and human consequences of downsizing and cost cutting measures (Gandolfi, 2009).

Economic and financial consequences

A multitude of studies have shown that most organisations in the public and private sectors have not been able to improve levels of efficiency, effectiveness, productivity, and profitability through downsizing. The downsizing literature even portrays an overwhelmingly negative picture of the financial benefits of downsizing, and there is strong evidence to suggest that a pure downsizing strategy is unlikely to be effective (Gandolfi, 2009).

OECD country experience suggests that without reviewing and reducing the functions of government (e.g. entitlement to services) through mechanisms such as strategic spending reviews, cuts to staffing levels is unlikely to meet service demands, and so ultimately staffing increases. Furthermore, cuts that are reactive and not driven by a longer-term strategy tend to result in short-term impact rather than transformational reforms that could allow sustainable staffing reductions.

At the macro level, OECD data suggest that, on average, the percentage of public employees has remained relatively stable. Although many OECD countries report sizeable reductions in central government employment, public sector employment as a percentage of total employment across OECD countries rose slightly between 2009 and 2013, from 21.1% to 21.3%, with small variation among OECD countries. The relative stability of this indicator seems to imply that any reduction in the public sector is matched by reductions of total employment in the private sector. In other words, public employment has been as responsive to the downturn as private employment. This indicator only captures reductions in the whole public sector, so it is possible that countries reporting high reductions in their CPAs make up for them in other areas or levels of public employment, such as direct service delivery and/or subnational levels. Nonetheless, it does not appear that the cost-driven reductions of public employment reported on in this survey have resulted in a significantly noticeable reduction pattern (and therefore sizeable savings) in the aggregate numbers for most OECD countries.

Figure 2.16. Public sector employment as a percentage of total employment (2013 and 2009)

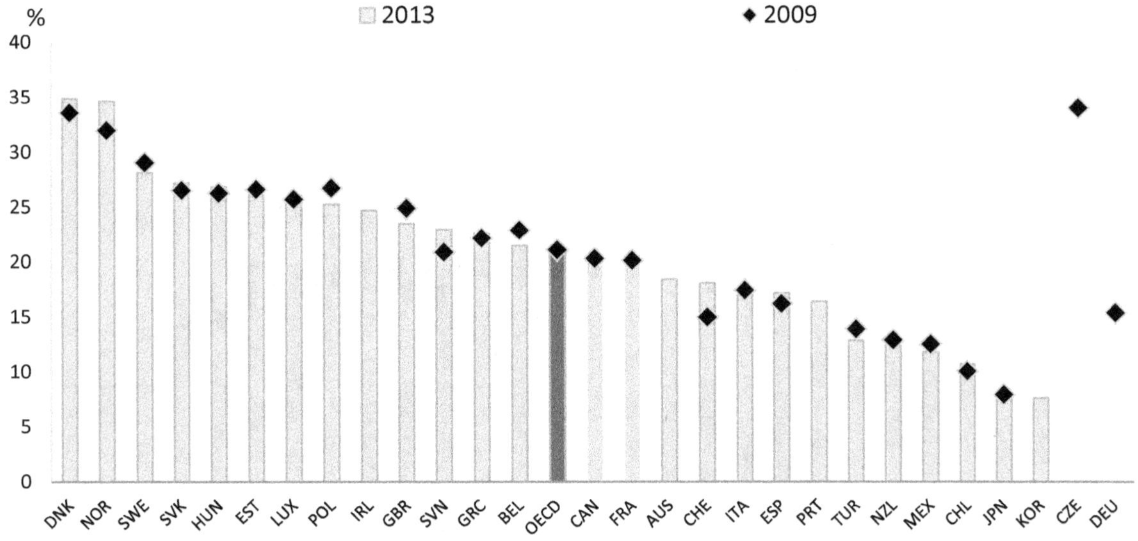

Source: OECD (2015), *Government at a Glance 2015*, OECD Publishing, Paris, http://dx.doi.org/10.1787/gov_glance-2015-en.

Notes: Data for Austria, Finland, Iceland, Israel, Korea, the Netherlands and the United States are not available. Data for Australia, Czech Republic, Germany, Ireland and Portugal are not included in the OECD average due to missing time series. Data for Czech Republic and New Zealand are expressed in full-time equivalents (FTEs). Data for Australia, Greece, Hungary, Slovenia and Spain and Ukraine are for 2012 rather than 2013. Data for Denmark, Luxembourg, New Zealand and Turkey are for 2011 rather than 2013. Data for Switzerland are for 2008 rather than 2009.

Compensation costs as percentage of GDP, captured in the OECD's national accounts data, can be another useful indicator. Here also the aggregate numbers remain relatively stable. Despite the efforts taken to cut government employment, readjust salaries and generate savings in training and other areas, it is not possible to point to a significant change in the aggregate.

Figure 2.17. Government production costs as a percentage of GDP (2007 and 2013)

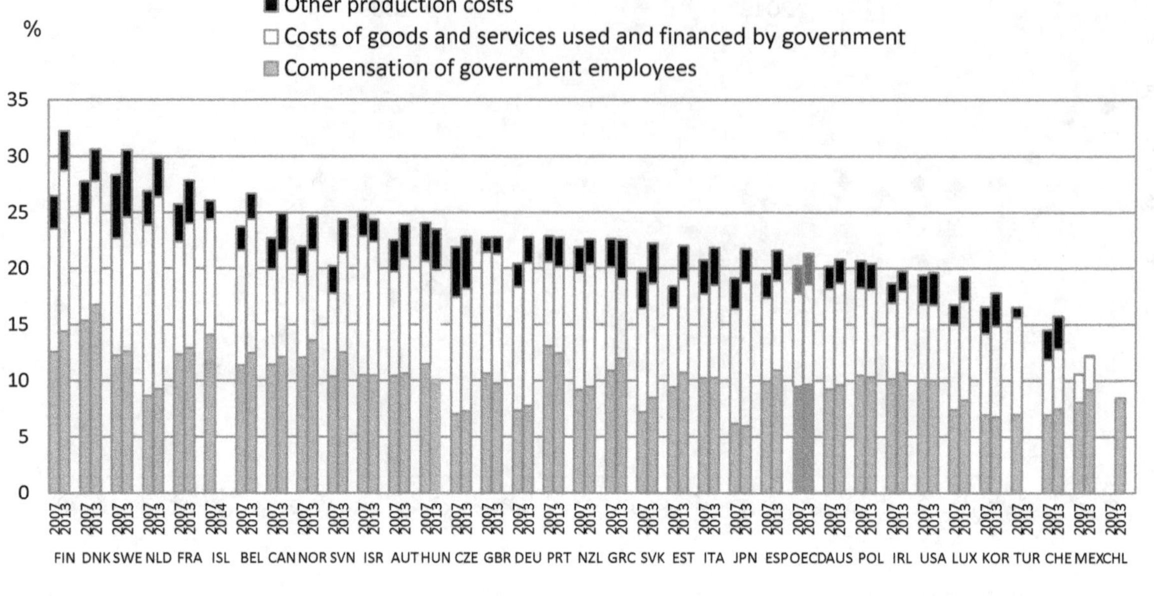

Source: OECD (2015), *Government at a Glance 2015*, OECD Publishing, Paris, http://dx.doi.org/10.1787/gov_glance-2015-en.

Notes: OECD National Accounts Statistics (database). Data for Australia are based on a combination of Government finance statistics and National Accounts data provided by the Australian Bureau of Statistics.Data for Turkey and are not included in the OECD average due to missing time-series. Data for Chile are available for compensation of employees only (Chile not included in the OECD average). The OECD average is weighted. Information on data for Israel: http://dx.doi.org/10.1787/888932315602

The stability of public employment and compensation costs at the macro level may hide savings in some governmental organisations at the micro level. Furthermore, the measures discussed in this part of the report may be partly responsible for public sector employment not rising following decreases in some country's private sectors. However, research has often demonstrated that downsizing contains significant costs in the medium- to long-term that are often overlooked by organisations of all kinds when pursuing workforce reductions. These may be particularly acute in the public sector, where contractual obligations often limit the speed of adjustment and often involve higher payments to redundant employees than in the private sector. Table 1.1 summarises many of the direct and indirect costs that need to be factored into all downsizing decisions.

Table 2.1. Employment downsizing and its alternatives: Direct and indirect costs of downsizing

Direct costs	Indirect costs
• Severance pay, in lieu of notice • Accrued vacation and sick pay • Supplemental unemployment benefits • Outplacement • Pension and benefits payouts • Administrative processing costs • Costs of rehiring former employees	• Recruiting and employment costs of new hires • Low morale, risk-averse survivors • Decreased productivity among survivors • Increase in unemployment tax rate • Lack of staff when economy rebounds • Start-up costs (recruiting, training, staffing) • Voluntary terminations of those who remain • Potential lawsuits from aggrieved employees • Potential strikes by unions in some countries • Loss of institutional memory and trust in management • Brand equity-cost-damage to the company's brand as an employer of choice

Source: Cascio, W. (2009), *Employment Downsizing and its Alternatives,* SHRM Foundation, www.shrm.org/about/foundation/products/documents/downsizing%20epg-%20final.pdf.

Organisational consequences

Downsizing is expected to create organisational, as well as financial, benefits. In the public sector, "anticipated organisational benefits include lower overheads, less bureaucracy, faster decision making, smoother communications, greater entrepreneurship, and increased productivity" (Burke and Cooper, 2000). However, most empirical findings suggest that the majority of restructuring and downsizing efforts fall short of objectives, and that implementation places heavy administrative burdens on organisations and managers. Overall, work demands increase significantly for middle managers during and after downsizing, and the downsizing tends to take priority over most other management challenges, such as innovation and other business improvements (Thornhill and Saunders, 1998).

Other organisational challenges may include a loss of capacity and corporate knowledge, which leaves with the employees. Many of the measures discussed above are also likely to have longer-term organisational capacity challenges. For example, hiring freezes, which are often the preferred method of workforce reductions, lead to an ageing of the workforce and reduces the diversity of ideas brought into the organisation. Reductions in training and development also reduce an organisation's ability to retool its workforce to meet new challenges. Salary reforms, if not carefully designed, limit the attractiveness of the few positions that are left open to recruitment, making it difficult to fill mission-critical occupations. In short, these measures may paralyse public organisations' abilities to evolve in the ways required of today's fast pace of change.

Human consequences

Little is known of what would happen to employees, and subsequently to the capacity of public sector organisations, if national governments continue to introduce significant pay cuts, decide on voluntary or obligatory job transfers, limit promotions, relax job security, reduce the scope of health schemes, and reform the standard employment model. The impact of these cost cutting measures on individual workplace behaviour is also unknown. Overall, the role and importance of changing emotions and fairness perceptions in the workplace, as a consequence of the introduction of reforms and austerity measures, is still widely under-researched (Cropanzano et al., 2011: 13).

From what is known in the academic field, compensation and benefit reductions and adjusted work schedules, which have a direct impact on an employee's personal finances, life, and livelihood, are most likely linked to increases in misconduct, disengagement and reduced work commitment. Overall, economic pressures, budgetary cuts, reduction in salaries and promotion opportunities may result in more stress, competition and a general decline in organisational culture (ethical climate). In these situations, principles such as fairness, courtesy, abuse of power and impartiality may be at risk. This can result in more ethical violations, such as stealing organisational resources, misconduct at work, and unwelcome behaviour. Job satisfaction and organisational commitment is negatively associated with overall perceptions of organisational and procedural injustice (for example unprofessional performance assessments and unfair recruitment decisions).

Justice perceptions have a significant role in predicting the effects of downsizing. People become demotivated and lose trust in leaders and the organisation if reforms are not perceived as fair. Therefore, how organisations handle the procedures related to downsizing, and how managers/supervisors treat employees before, during and after the downsizing, is very important in predicting survivors' attitudinal and behavioural responses. "Survivors" expect a fair procedure and fair treatment from the organisation. When this expectation of fairness is not met, they perceive the organisation as not fulfilling their obligation (Arshada and Sparrow, 2010).

Box 2.6. Survivor syndrome

The effects of downsizing extend far beyond those who lose their jobs. Downsizing has implications for management, HRM departments, staff representatives, survivors, organisational culture and trust levels. Studies have shown that downsizing affects job commitment levels, job satisfaction, stress and health levels and morale. Two concepts are central to understanding this: the psychological contract and organisational justice perceptions (Cascio, 2010).

Many studies (e.g. OECD, 2011) have shown that downsizing has serious and negative effects on the public service workforce in terms of trust in the organisation, leadership, morale, job satisfaction, and job engagement etc. According to Gandolfi: "Downsizing scholars have identified and empirically studied the symptoms associated with the emotions, behaviours, and attitudes of survivors (i.e. those who retain their jobs after downsizing). These symptoms have come to be known as 'sicknesses'. The most prominent sickness, the survivor syndrome, is a set of emotions, behaviours, and attitudes exhibited by surviving employees. Brockner (1998) asserts that downsizing engenders a variety of psychological states in survivors, namely, guilt, positive inequity, anger, relief, and job insecurity. These mental states have the potential to influence the survivors' work behaviours and attitudes, such as motivation, commitment, satisfaction, and job performance. The survivor syndrome is characterised by decreased levels of morale, employee involvement, work productivity, and trust towards management" (Gandofi, 2009: 409).

Sources: Cascio, W. (2010), "Downsizing and redundancy", in Wilkinson, A. N. Bacon, T. Redman and S. Snell (eds.), *The SAGE handbook of human resource management*, pp. 336-349, SAGE Publications Ltd, London, http://dx.doi.org/10.4135/9780857021496.n20.

OECD (2011), *Public Servants as Partners for Growth: Toward a Stronger, Leaner and More Equitable Workforce*, OECD Publishing, Paris. DOI: http://dx.doi.org/10.1787/9789264166707-en.

Brockner, J., (1988). "The effects of work layoffs in survivors: research, theory and practice", *Research in Organizational Behavior*, Vol. 10, pp. 213-255.

Gandolfi, F. (2009), "Unravelling Downsizing – What do we know about the Phenomenon?", *Review of International Comparative Management*, Vol. 10/3.

The relationship between downsizing and stress is well established. Many countries report trends towards more job intensity and higher stress levels; almost no country reports decreasing levels of stress and job intensity. Thus, rising stress levels and job intensity appear to be global trends.

Figure 2.18. Development of job intensity and stress (percent of responding countries) (2008-2013)

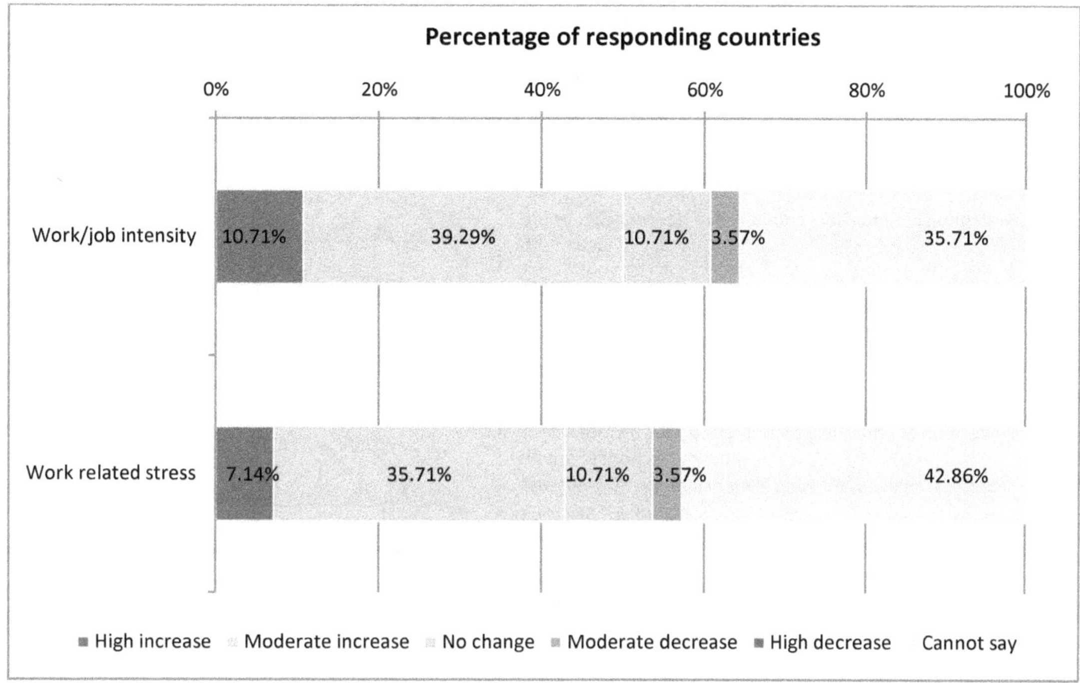

Source: OECD (2014b), Question 22, *Survey on Managing Budgeting Constraints: Implications for HRM and Employment in Central Public Administration*, OECD, Paris, www.oecd.org/gov/pem/2014-human-resource-management-survey.pdf.

Evidence from this survey appears to indicate that the development of stress levels, job intensity, and sickness levels is highly contextual and not linked to budgetary challenges. While the survey cannot determine the reasons for these increases, they could be a cause for concern as these trends are likely to show more side effects, such as higher turnover rates, higher sickness rates, lower productivity levels, less job satisfaction and less job engagement.

More job intensity and more stress are not necessarily a problem as long as job control, job autonomy and job engagement are also increasing. However, when rising job intensity and stress levels are linked to more workload, less job control and more job constraints, problems may occur. In such situations, stress and work intensity may have negative impacts on workplace behaviour and attitudes.

A study by Demmke and Moilanen (2012) shows a strong relationship between the introduction of austerity measures and workplace attitudes in EU central administrations, in particular a lowering of job satisfaction, trust in leadership, workplace commitment and loyalty. This OECD survey confirms the Demmke/Moilanen findings. Overall, many countries report a decrease of trust in their own organisation and in leadership, and decreasing job commitment and job satisfaction as a result of the implementation of new cost cutting measures.

Figure 2.19. Effects of cost cutting measures on workplace behaviour (percent of responding countries) (2008-2013)

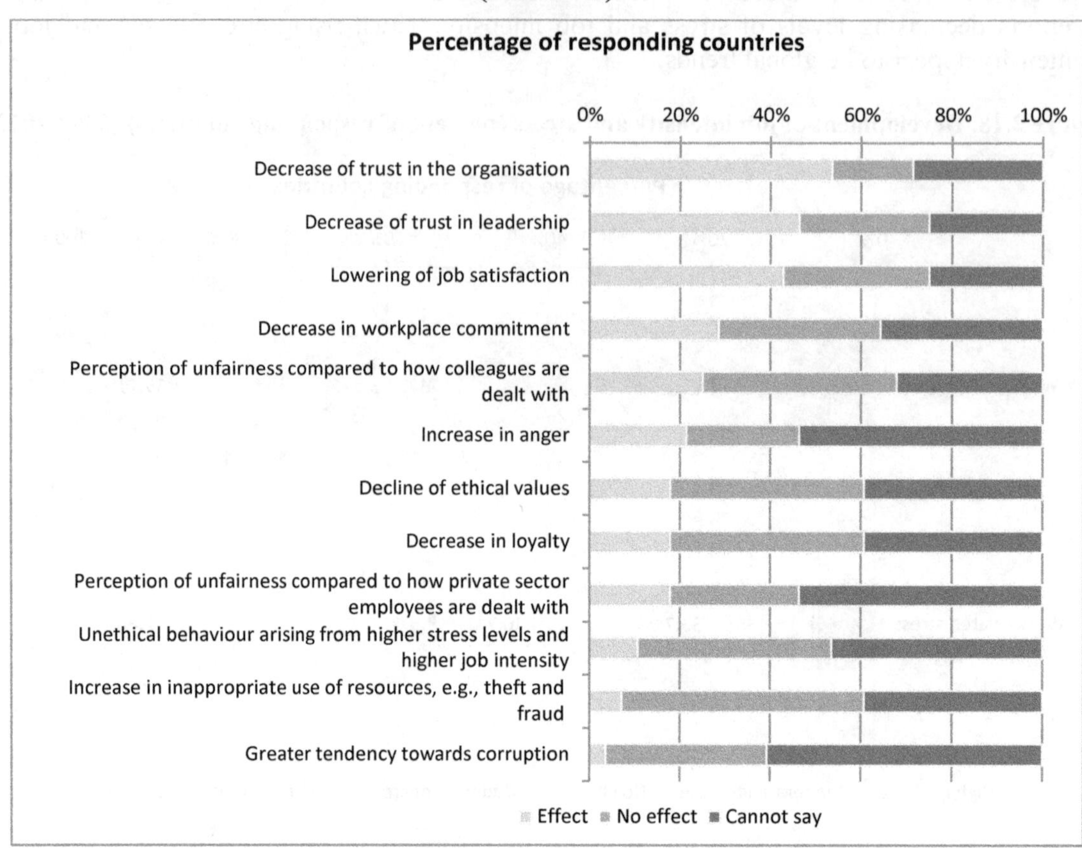

Source: OECD (2014b), Question 20, *Survey on Managing Budgeting Constraints: Implications for HRM and Employment in Central Public Administration*, OECD, Paris, www.oecd.org/gov/pem/2014-human-resource-management-survey.pdf.

Countries that report the most negative effects on workplace behaviour are also generally countries with higher budgetary pressures. This is mostly the case in relation to trust levels in the organisation, trust levels in leadership, workplace commitment, job satisfaction and the increase in anger. However, the data does not show strong increases in unethical behaviour, which seems to point to the continued importance of values and a strong public sector ethos.

The data do not allow for a more detailed analysis of the impact of HRM measures on different categories of employees, for example, the differences regarding technical staff and top managers. In this regard, the empirical evidence is scarce. In their study on the impact of cutbacks and job satisfaction of top managers, van der Voet and van de Walle (2014) concluded that the job satisfaction of top managers is declining, but for different reasons than for other public employees. According to the authors, "cutback measures are negatively related to the perceived managerial autonomy of public managers and positively to the degree in which politicians interfere in the affairs of managers, autonomy may function as a mechanism to explain decreased job satisfaction as a result of cutback implementation." (van der Voet and van de Walle, 2014)

Overall, the answers of many countries reveal some worrying trends that warrant an investigation of the effects of current cost cutting measures. Deteriorations could be noted in the following HRM policies:

- Negative effects of downsizing policies
- Increase in stress
- Negative impact of cuts to compensation (less pay, less motivational pay)
- Reduced career opportunities and reduced promotion opportunities and policies
- Negative effects of cutting training policies on skill levels
- Increased job intensity
- Decreasing attractiveness of public sector employment

In an increasing number of countries, officials are dissatisfied with restricted career opportunities and slow advancement in the hierarchies. Restricted promotion opportunities show that organisational change is most easily accomplished when the people affected have something to gain. However, under conditions of budgetary pressures, the acceptance of change will be unlikely as there is little to win. "Under these conditions, creativity diminishes, innovation and risk taking decline, and the sense of excitement that comes from doing new things disappears. Simply put, it just is not as much fun working and managing in a contracting organisation as it is in an expanding one" (Levine, 1979: 180).

Impacts on public employment and the civil service

In the first edition of *Civil Services in the Europe of 15*, the authors came to the conclusion that the differences in the working conditions between civil servants, public employees and private sector employees were becoming less pronounced (Auer et al., 1996). This trend continues. Today, the most important differences relate mostly to job security, recruitment procedures, pay systems and career development policies. However, even these features are undergoing tremendous changes: job security is being reduced, recruitment procedures are being made more flexible, pay systems are individualised, and career structures are modified and, in some cases, even abolished. As a consequence, civil service employment differs less from private sector employment than ever before. Although the differences between civil service employment and public service employment are becoming less clear, the challenges faced by the public sector are perhaps more pronounced than ever, meaning that the kind of employment system required to meet these challenges should be explored

In many OECD countries, job security levels differ amongst public law civil servants and labour law public employees. Consequently, countries with high budgetary pressures have focused on the relaxation of job security for public employees. In most of these countries, dismissals have become easier for public employees, but not for civil servants.

These figures suggest that despite alignment trends between the public and private sector and amongst civil servants and other public employees, differences in job security are increasing amongst the various employment categories. This is mostly the case in countries with high budgetary pressures, due to the focus on dismissing public employees rather than civil servants.

Central administrations may be increasingly confronted with growing inconsistencies regarding the employment status and the employment of public employees in civil service employment positions. Fixed-term employees may be the first to find themselves impacted by downsizing measures, however, there also appears to be a desire to increase the flexibility of civil service employment and to replace civil servants by fixed-term employees. Twelve countries have indicated a need for more flexible employment in order to save resources. Nine countries replied that the use of fixed-term employment is a consequence of budgetary constraints.

Figure 2.20. Main reasons for the use of fixed-term employees (number of countries) (2008-2013)

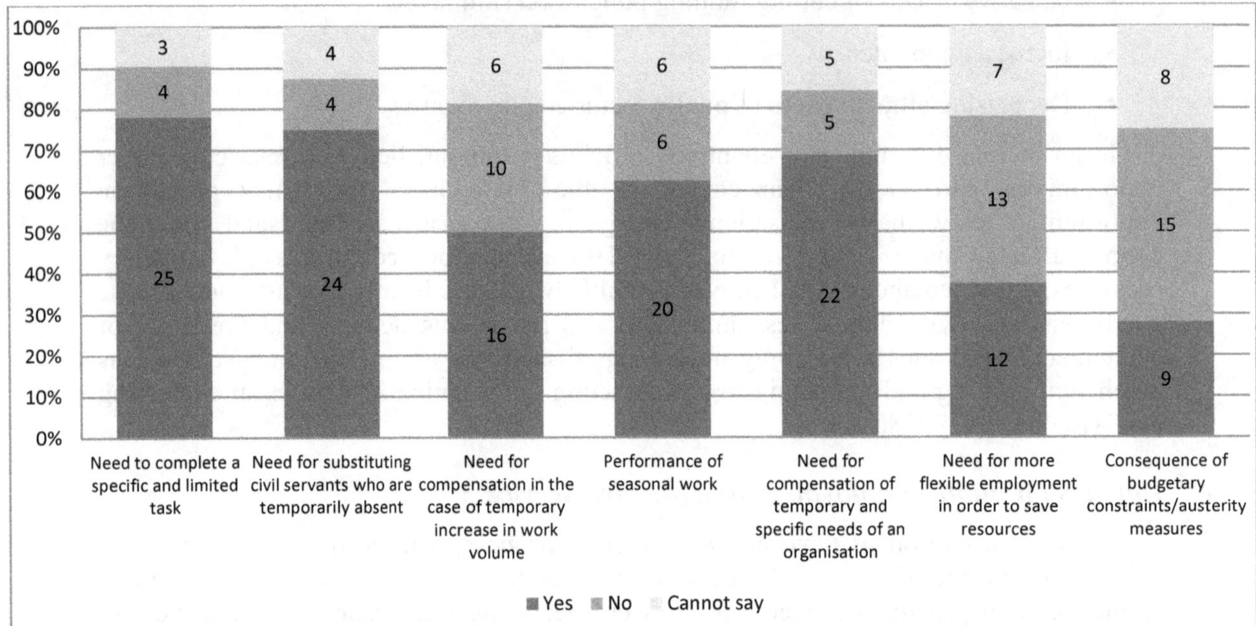

Source: OECD (2014b), Question 24, *Survey on Managing Budgeting Constraints: Implications for HRM and Employment in Central Public Administration*, OECD, Paris, www.oecd.org/gov/pem/2014-human-resource-management-survey.pdf.

In response to the survey question: "Will budgetary constraints and the subsequent need for stabilising national economies be an extra impetus to abolishing employment as civil servants?", 6 of the 23 countries who responded answered with "very much" (Australia, Hungary, Spain, Greece, Belgium, Canada) and another 6 with "somewhat" (Estonia, Slovenia, the United Kingdom, Poland, Mexico, Korea).

While a number of countries with high budgetary pressures responded positively to this question, the constitutional, legal, cultural and political context appears to play a significant determining factor. For example, in Germany, the German Constitution (*Grundgesetz*) requires the existence of a specific civil service. Portugal and Italy, however, have already reformed the civil service status. Sweden does not see a need to abolish the civil service, as differences between civil servants and private sector employees (almost) do not exist anymore, an example which suggests that it is possible to have a functioning and modern civil service within a private law employment framework when specific values and culture are reinforced through management actions. These actions will be discussed in more detail in the second part of this report.

The overall trends described in this section reinforce a running theme in this first part of the report: reforms and reductions can only be sustained when they are linked to a strategy and driven by principle. While some countries see the relaxation of job security among some categories as a way of improving workforce agility, developing public sector skills, and responding to forecasted changing needs, many appear to be primarily driven by reactive measures. The OECD is working with member countries to identify common principles that may help to guide the transformation of public employment in a sustainable and effective manner.

Box 2.7. Should public HRM policies be different to private sector HRM policies

There has been ongoing discussion in the scientific community for many decades about the differences between public and private organisations, and the impact of HRM reforms on individual workplace behaviour, status, work motivation and character traits. The idea that public organisations are different was always in striking contrast to the opinion of major public administration experts, such as Herbert Simon and Max Weber, who underlined the commonalities among organisations and suggested that public and private organisations are more alike than different.

Proponents of maintaining differences between public and private sector employees argue that work in the public service is specific and, by nature, different from work in the private sector. Consequently, civil servants should also be treated differently because they:

- Work to multiple complex objectives, which make performance management difficult.
- Are given considerable power and responsibilities.
- Set legal and normative standards for citizens.
- Have a responsibility to provide leadership.
- May intervene directly in the basic rights of citizens, e.g. police.
- Are financed and paid from the public budget in order to carry out work for the public.
- Have different values, ethos and (public sector) motivation.

For proponents of "differences" amongst public and private sector organisations, and between civil servants and private sector employees, the specific public tasks also require specific working conditions and, in some cases, a specific legal status that links the person to the state. In particular, employees who are directly participating in the exercise of powers, who are intervening in the fundamental rights of citizens, who spend public money and who are safeguarding the general interest of the state (or of other public authorities) should have a specific status that binds them to the public interest. It is important to clearly define the categories and posts that fall within these categories. Today, countries apply very different definitions to the term "civil service" or to posts exercising public powers.

Opponents of a specific civil service status and specific HRM features argue that the tasks of civil servants are not more specific or more valuable than those carried out in the private sector. In addition, critics of traditional civil services point to the disadvantages of traditional career civil services. Their arguments can be summarised as follows:

- Even if public tasks are specific, this does not require a specific civil service status or specific legal contractual status. For example, any specific requirements can be easily arranged in an ordinary employment law contract (which is often based on collective agreements). The terms "essential functions of the state" and "safeguarding the general interest" are difficult to interpret.

Box 2.7. Should public HRM policies be different to private sector HRM policies *(continued)*

- It is not possible to argue that civil servants carry out more important tasks than private employees. Are doctors, workers in chemical companies, nuclear power station employees, farmers, banks and biotechnology staff not carrying out public interest tasks?
- Many current reform trends reveal an enormous paradox in several states with a specific career system. In these countries, working processes, working conditions and organisational structures are different in private and public organisations. However, there is very little evidence that the actual behaviour of public employees differs from those working in the private sector.
- In some countries, civil servants carry out exactly the same tasks and functions as public employees who do not have the civil service status (and sometimes work in the same organisation and the same office). However, performance level and ethical behaviour are actually the same whereas working conditions differ.

Judging which arguments are "better" should be linked to an understanding of the national context and administrative tradition. However, current trends are relatively clear in most countries: many experts in the field point to the growing difficulties in identifying clear differences between the two sectors in terms of governance, outsourcing, public-private partnerships and consultancy, and argue that there has been too little sound analysis of the real differences between public and private organisations (and public and private sector employees) in the 21st century.

Sources: Demmke, C. and T. Moilanen (2010), *Civil Services in the EU of 27*, Peter Lang, Frankfurt.

Demmke, C. and T. Moilanen (2012), *Effectiveness of Public Service Ethics and Good Governance*, Peter Lang, Frankfurt.

Demmke, C. and T. Moilanen (2013), Governmental Transformation and the Future of Public Employment, Peter Lang, Frankfurt.

Potential opportunities of budgetary constraints

The cost cutting focus of the measures described above are somewhat counterbalanced by a belief among senior HRM officials that budgetary pressures in the period after 2008 also produce opportunities for better and more forward looking HRM reform. One opportunity is the possibility to improve workforce planning and to improve data management practices. Another opportunity is to better anticipate demographic changes and become more professional and more strategic in anticipating future HRM and employment requirements.

Acting on these opportunities requires a strategic vision of the role of HRM in the future in order to drive planning. This will mean taking stock of the role of civil servants and the skills and qualities that will be required to meet challenges emerging from the economic crisis and well beyond. The civil service will need be an attractive employer, by actively managing the well-being of its employees and reinforcing its employer brand. This means planning reforms that treat employees as skilled professionals, and not only as costs to be minimised. In this report, and in those to come, the OECD will address each of these opportunities and consider the underlying principles that are required to support forward-looking civil services in terms of skills, diversity, employment conditions and planning implications.

Figure 2.21. Positive opportunities of budgetary constraints (percent of responding countries) (2008-2013)

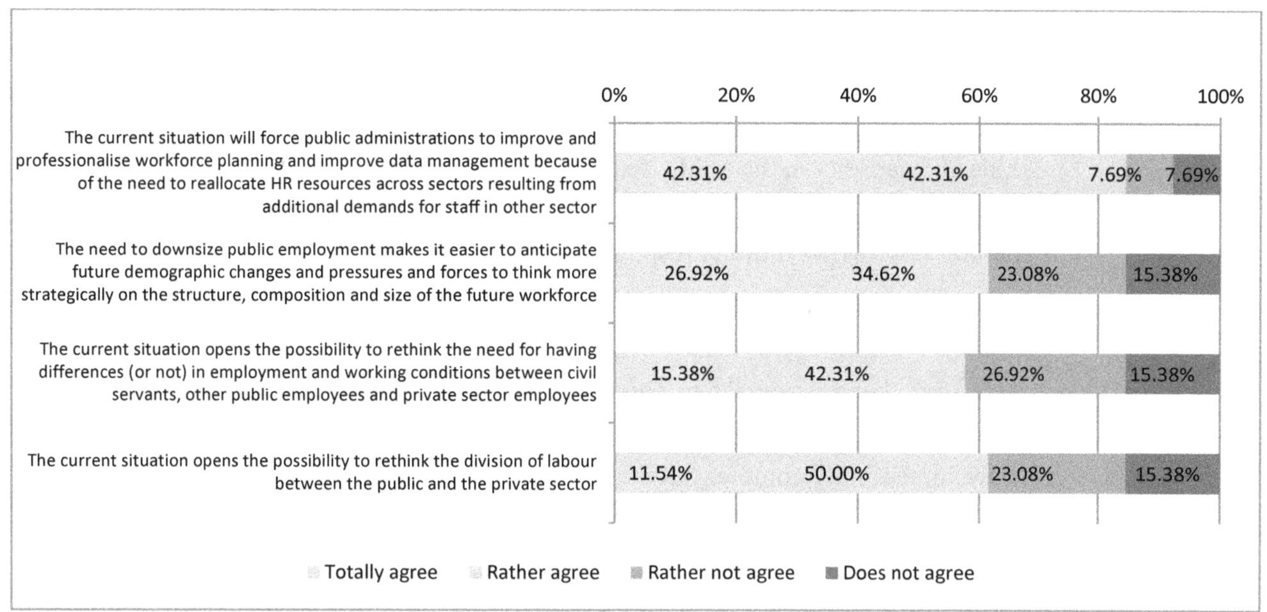

Source: OECD (2014b), Question 24, *Survey on Managing Budgeting Constraints: Implications for HRM and Employment in Central Public Administration*, OECD, Paris, www.oecd.org/gov/pem/2014-human-resource-management-survey.pdf.

Concluding questions: What impacts in the longer term?

Chapter 2 has shown that countries are implementing many cost reduction measures in the field of HRM. HRM policies in most OECD countries are moving through a fascinating, but also a disorienting period. Whereas past organisational reform trends were characterised by a move away from the classical bureaucratic model, current reforms do not indicate convergence towards a new administrative best-practice model. There are several reform trajectories in the field of HRM that lead to a modernisation of structures, processes and employment conditions, but these highlight the existence of alternative models rather than a shift towards one common HRM reform model. There is no common trend towards one employment model.

The survey results presented in Chapter 2 may raise more questions than can be answered. Some of the most pressing are the following:

- Government needs employment systems that guarantee adherence to the core values and administrative law principles, and that ensure a focus on effectiveness, efficiency and accountability. Governments must ensure equal treatment and fairness, while ensuring the merit principle and the equality of chances.
  - What tension does this raise for government employment in times of downsizing?
  - How are countries balancing the need to manage budgetary constraints while ensuring the principles of justice and fairness regarding, for example, diversity and inclusion?
  - Is the public sector still a model employer in this respect?

- This survey illustrates worrying trends in the field of training and skills development. Whereas in the past, civil servants were experts who held diplomas and received little training, today civil servants are required to continuously develop their skills and competencies.
  - What impact are the measures identified in this survey expected to have on skills and capacity in the public sector?
  - Have any long-term considerations been taken into account when designing training reforms? Is training responding to new skills needs?
  - Have dismissals been conducted with a sense of longer-term planning and skills retention?
  - Have there been processes to encourage knowledge transfer from those who opt for early retirement?
- CPAs are increasingly complex. In the future, the central workforce will likely be smaller, more mobile, better qualified and more diverse than ever before. And while the expectations of what the government can provide are increasing, the resources available to meet these expectations are diminishing. Civil servants of the future will likely face more job intensity, stress, complexity and flexibility. They will have to be comfortable with change and innovation. At the same time they will likely take more autonomous decisions, be more responsible, accountable, performance-oriented, and subject to new competency and skill requirements.
  - Have cost cutting measures in the field of HRM been designed in a way to help rather than hinder the civil services of OECD countries to meet these new challenges and take on these new roles?
  - Many of the measures discussed here are effective short-term fixes to budgetary constraints, but will they have longer-term consequences? How can these be tracked?
  - How can long-term success be measured?

If budgetary constraints persist, it is likely that levels of job satisfaction, job commitment, trust in the organisation and trust in leadership will further decline in many OECD countries. Countries are advised to identify measures to counter these developments; otherwise the delivery of effective public policies will eventually be at risk.

According to Peters and Pierre, "the challenge in the longer term...is to design organisations that combine the efficiency and service capacity of decentralised organisations with the uniform and legalistic nature of hierarchical organisations" (Peters and Pierre, 2003: 6). The task ahead is not an easy one: save resources while introducing "smart" austerity measures, create innovative workplaces, reform and modernise work systems and professionalise HRM policies. Most of these can only be done together with employees, and not in a top-down manner imposed on employees. If organisations want engaged motivated and committed employees they must accept that "employee engagement is best seen as an outcome of managerial activity to build perceptions of trust, fairness and organisational justice...The question remains on how trust, fairness and justice are built" (Purcell, 2012: 13). Unfortunately, HRM policies in times of budgetary constraints appear to result in less trust.

Some countries have started to combine cost cutting measures with reforms intended to address the human side of public employment. Reforms are primarily intended to ensure that the motivation and commitment of employees is retained through different employee and union engagement measures, and measures that counteract the so-called survivor syndrome. Linking these reforms in the context of deliberate and sober workforce planning begins to clarify how countries can approach workforce restructuring in response to the crisis in ways that may minimise the negative impacts and result in "responsible restructuring". Leadership, values and engagement can be reinforced through engagement surveys and leadership development innovative work systems and HR policies can be strengthened through training, networks, and increased use of alternative working methods workforce planning and agile HRM systems can help to identify, attract and allocate the right skills across the workforce. Chapter 3 of this report looks more specifically at employee engagement, which provides a counterbalance to many of the worrying trends identified in Chapter 2.

References

Arshada, R. and P. Sparrow (2010), "Downsizing and survivor reactions in Malaysia: modelling antecedents and outcomes of psychological contract violation", *The International Journal of Human Resource Management*, Vol. 21, No. 11, p. 1793.

Auer, A., C. Demmke and R. Polet (1996), *Civil Services in the Europe of Fifteen: Current Situation and Prospects*, European Institute of Public Administration, Maastricht.

Bach, S. and I. Kessler (2012), *The Modernisation of the Public Services and Employee Relations*, Palgrave, Hampshire.

Bossaert, D. et al. (2008), *Training and Human Resource Development in the European Union Member States*, European Institute of Public Administration, Maastricht.

Brockner, J., (1988). "The effects of work layoffs in survivors: research, theory and practice", *Research in Organizational Behavior*, Vol. 10, pp. 213-255.

Cropanzano, R., J.H. Stein and T. Nadisc (2011), *Social justice and the experience of emotion*, Routledge, New York.

Cascio, W. (2010), "Downsizing and redundancy", in Wilkinson, A. N. Bacon, T. Redman and S. Snell (eds.), *The SAGE handbook of human resource management*, pp. 336-349, SAGE Publications Ltd, London, http://dx.doi.org/10.4135/9780857021496.n20.

Cascio, W. (2009), *Employment Downsizing and its Alternatives*, SHRM Foundation, www.shrm.org/about/foundation/products/documents/downsizing%20epg-%20final.pdf.

Cascio, W. (2005), "Strategies for Responsible Restructuring", *Academy of Management Executive*, 2005, Vol. 19, No. 4.

Demmke, C. (2009), Leistungsbezahlung in den öffentlichen Diensten der EU-Mitgliedstaaten – eine Reformbaustelle, in: *der moderne Staat*, No. 1

Demmke, C. and T. Moilanen (2013), *Governmental Transformation and the Future of Public Employment*, Peter Lang, Frankfurt.

Demmke, C. and T. Moilanen (2012), *Effectiveness of Public Service Ethics and Good Governance*, Peter Lang, Frankfurt.

Demmke, C. and T. Moilanen (2010), *Civil Services in the EU of 27*, Peter Lang, Frankfurt.

Ferlie, E., L. Lynn and C. Pollitt (2007), "Introductory Remarks", *The Oxford Handbook of Public Management*, Oxford University Press.

Gandolfi, F. (2009), "Unravelling Downsizing – What do we know about the Phenomenon?", *Review of International Comparative Management*, Vol. 10/3.

Gupta, N. and J.D. Shaw, (2014), "Employee compensation: The neglected area of HRM research", *Human Resource Management Review*, Vol. 24, pp. 1-4.

Kellough, E. and L. Nigro (2002), "Pay for Performance in Georgia State Government", *Review of Public Personnel Administration*, Vol. 22, No. 2, pp. 146-166.

Levine, C.H. (1979), "More on Cutback Management: Hard Questions for Hard Times", *Public Administration Review*, Vol. 39, No. 2, p. 179-183.

Metsma, M. (2014), "The Impact of Cutback Management on Civil-Service Training: The Case of Estonia", *Administrative Culture*, Vol. 15/1, pp. 58-79.

OECD (2016), *HRM survey (Managing Budgeting Constraints Implications for HRM and Employment in Central Public Administration)*, OECD, Paris, http://qdd.oecd.org/subject.aspx?Subject=985A031D-9D64-4E13-B46F-2189F2447481.

OECD (2015), *Government at a Glance 2015*, OECD Publishing, Paris, http://dx.doi.org/10.1787/gov_glance-2015-en.

OECD (2014a), *OECD Economic Outlook, Volume 2014 Issue 1*, OECD Publishing, Paris, http://dx.doi.org/10.1787/eco_outlook-v2014-1-en.

OECD (2014b), *Survey on Managing Budgeting Constraints: Implications for HRM and Employment in Central Public Administration*, OECD, Paris, www.oecd.org/gov/pem/2014-human-resource-management-survey.pdf.

OECD (2012), *Restoring Public Finances, 2012 Update*, OECD Publishing, Paris, http://dx.doi.org/10.1787/9789264179455-en.

OECD (2011), *Public Servants as Partners for growth: Towards a Stronger, Leaner and More Equitable Workforce*, OECD Publishing, Paris, DOI: http://dx.doi.org/10.1787/9789264166707-en

Perry, J., T.A. Engbers and S.Y. Jun (2009), "Back to the Future? Performance Related Pay, Empirical research, and the Perils of Persistance", *Public Administration Review*, Vol. 69, No. 1, pp. 39-51.

Peters G. and J. Pierre (eds), (2003), *Handbook of Public Administration*, Second edition, Sage.

Pollitt C. and G. Bouckaert (2011), *Public Management Reform: A Comparative Analysis - New Public Management, Governance, and the Neo-Weberian State*, Third edition, Oxford University Press.

Purcell, J. (2012), "The limits and possibilities of employee engagement", *Warwick Papers in Industrial Relations*, University of Warwick, No. 96.

Stewart G.L. and K.G. Brown (2011), *Human Resource Management, Second edition*, John Wiley, New Baskerville.

Taylor, J. and L. Beh (2013), "The Impact of Pay-for-Performance Schemes on the Performance of Australian and Malaysian Government Employees", *Public Management Review*, Vol. 15, No. 8, pp.1090-1115.

Thornhill, A. and M.N.K. Suanders (1998), "The meanings, consequences and implications of the management of downsizing and redundancy: a review", *Saunders Personnel Review*, Vol. 27 No. 4, p. 289.

van der Voet, J. and S. van de Walle (2014), *How cutbacks and job satisfaction are related: The role of top-level public managers' autonomy*, FP7 COCOPS Final Academic Conference, Leuven, Belgium.

Chapter 3.

An engaged civil service for innovation, productivity and sustainable reform

This chapter looks at how a number of OECD countries are using the concept of employee engagement to drive a better, evidence-based approach to management. Definitions and evidence of engagement are discussed, followed by a description of how the United States, the United Kingdom and the German Employment Agency (Bundesagentur fur Arbeit, BA) measure engagement and use it to drive performance. This is followed by a discussion of how the tools of leadership and management can promote engagement, as well as a modern and individualised HRM. Chapter 3 concludes with suggestions on how engagement can be improved in OECD civil services.

Introduction

It is likely that budgetary pressures will continue to have a strong impact on human resource management (HRM) reform agendas. Ensuring sustainable performance in this context requires HRM policies that look at people, and not just employment numbers, in order to ensure government performance and public sector innovation. If the interest is only in short-term cost cutting, many of the measures discussed in Chapter 2 may well be helping to achieve that goal. But if the interest is in organisational performance and building long-term capacity for innovation and resilience, complementary elements of HRM toolkits need to be utilised.

The strategic orientation of HRM, and the need to adopt dynamic employment policies (OECD, 2011), is playing an increasingly important role in supporting sustainable reform efforts in public administrations. Public administrations need employees who not only identify strongly with their job tasks as contributors to public value, but who also identify strongly with their employer and its organisational goals. This can improve innovative capacity, boost workforce productivity and help to implement reforms on a sustainable basis. In modern work settings, it is important that employees are supported to work with their whole capacity. This suggests a need for strategies that take into account the needs and expectations of a diverse and, in part, ageing workforce.

Employee engagement is a concept that describes and measures the link between employees, the work they do and the organisations within which they work. Engaged employees are those who are "committed to their organisation's goals and values, motivated to contribute to organisational success, and are able at the same time to enhance their own sense of well-being." (MacLeod and Clarke, 2011: 9) Empirical evidence links employee engagement and related concepts of organisational commitment and staff motivation to better organisational outcomes, including: efficiency, productivity, public sector innovation, citizen trust in public sector institutions, and employee trust in organisational leadership. Employee engagement strengthens organisational capacity as it is positively related to individual performance and employee retention. Employee engagement is based on trust within organisations, and, as such, can be hard to build and easy to break, especially during times of austerity, as shown in the OECD survey explored in Chapter 2.

Employee engagement, measured through carefully designed employee surveys, provides a data-driven approach to track and benchmark the performance of organisational leadership, people management, and HRM, and inform policies and reforms in these areas. According to many of the leading practitioners in this field, engagement can be measured at both an individual and an organisational level, and this can provide evidence-based insight into the organisational culture and health of an organisation. OECD work in this area addresses a trend that is intended to support evidence-based public management and identify concrete measures to strengthen organisational performance.

This work is based on a number of OECD country examples that take into account different cultural contexts. They all have the common goal of finding new ways to improve leadership and collaboration, and of developing a positive and inclusive workplace climate. These illustrate the strategic value afforded to promoting employee engagement. It will be essential to learn from examples of good practice, while keeping in mind the specific needs, capacities and context of each administration.

The case studies illustrate how effective leadership, middle management and collaboration promote staff engagement, which, in turn, is the basis from which to promote innovation and from which to contribute to public value and trust in public administration. This is important, as public organisations are essential for creating relationships between individuals and society. The state allocates resources, distributes goods and services, and contributes to stable economic growth (Musgrave, 1959, as cited in Meynhardt and Bartholomes, 2011), but it also creates (or destroys) the legitimacy of trust in public action (Rainey, 2003, as cited in Meynhardt and Bartholomes, 2011).

Why employee engagement matters

What does engagement mean?

In literature and in practice, there are various definitions, meanings, measurements and theories of employee engagement (Saks and Gruman, 2014). The common thread is a focus on how to positively influence employee behaviour by aligning goals and values. This provides an important and complementary counter-balance to performance regimes based on regulation and compliance, which often prove costly, ineffective and slow.

The concept of work engagement refers to goal-directed action in line with the organisation's goals. An engaged employee will gear her or his behaviour towards achieving these goals as effectively as possible. Motivation and decision making are therefore two processes that underlie engagement.

One commonly used definition refers to engagement as an active, positive and fulfilling work-related state of mind that is characterised by vigour, dedication and absorption (Schaufeli and Bakker, 2004). Guest (2015) refers to the European model that focuses on attitudes. The American approach focuses on motivational aspects viewed as a mediating variable between inputs and outcomes: physical, emotional and cognitive engagement (Guest, 2015).

Employees with high levels of engagement tend to:

- contribute to innovation by involving themselves and their ideas in their work (Salanova and Schaufeli, 2008, Bakker, 2009; 2011).
- strengthen resilience and self-initiative by asking for feedback and support, if needed (Bakker, 2009; 2011).
- work energetically without suffering from burnout (Schaufeli and Bakker, 2010). This is relevant for well-being and mental health in the workplace, and healthy leadership.
- be able to detach from work (Sonnentag, Binnewies and Mojza, 2010). This is relevant for HR policies that focus on the reconciliation of work and family, work-life balance and corporate health management.

Engagement can, therefore, contribute to health promotion in the workplace and healthy leadership. It is not about considering why people suffer from burnout and preventing this, or reducing the risk; instead, it is about considering how engagement and health can be promoted, and therefore how actions can be preventative instead of reactive. This can result in cost savings as sick leave often results in the loss of working capacities and high costs.

Box 3.1. The difference between job satisfaction and work engagement

Within the framework of occupational psychology research, investigations have been made into job satisfaction. However, this concept must be distinguished from work engagement.

Job satisfaction is related to work engagement because both constructs encompass an emotional aspect of the working activity (Rich, 2006), but a distinction must nevertheless be drawn between the two.

Whereas work engagement relates to individual behaviour and involvement in work, the expression of job satisfaction reflects an evaluation of how the desired and actual working conditions compare to one another. Job satisfaction can therefore be seen as a stance on or attitude to the work and its conditions, with regard to whether the work is conducive to the fulfilment of relevant needs (von Rosenstiel, Molt and Rüttinger, 2005).

Satisfaction does not automatically entail active participation and exertion of energy (Rich, 2006), so there is also a risk of inertia or maintaining an existing status quo. This can explain the weak direct relationships between job satisfaction and productivity (Vroom, 1964; Petty, McGee and Cavender, 1984; Iaffaldano and Muchinsky, 1985; Judge et al., 2001). Furthermore, the findings are not clear, since even less-satisfied employees perform their function when they work to rule (i.e. when they perform to their expected level).

This demonstrates that the concept of engagement is distinct: engaged employees participate beyond the expected level and contribute actively to the success of the organisation.

Sources:

Rich, B.L. (2006), *Job engagement: Construct validation and relationships with job satisfaction, job involvement, and intrinsic motivation,* Gainesville, University of Florida, http://www.gbv.de/dms/zbw/583845355.pdf

von Rosenstiel, L., W. Molt and B. Rüttinger (2005), *Organisationspsychologie* (9th completely revised and expanded ed.), Kohlhammer, Stuttgart.

Vroom, V.H. (1964), *Work and motivation*, Wiley, New York.

Petty, M.M., G.W. McGee and J.W. Cavender (1984), "A meta-analysis of the relationships between individual job satisfaction and individual performance", in *The Academy of Management Review*, Vol. 9, No. 4, pp. 712-721.

Iaffaldano, M.T. and P.M Muchinsky (1985), "Job satisfaction and job performance: A meta-analysis", *Psychological Bulletin*, Vol. 97, No. 2, pp.251-273.

Judge, T.A., C.J. Thoresen, J.E. Bono and G.K. Patton (2001), "The job satisfaction - job performance relationship: A qualitative and quantitative review", *Psychological Bulletin,* Vol. 127, No.3, pp. 376-407.

In summary, it can be concluded that engaged employees feel a sense of belonging to their organisation and duties, are motivated to involve themselves, and report increased satisfaction with their work and working conditions. As a concept, it goes beyond the measurement of satisfaction by including aspects of commitment to organisational values and goals, and linking behaviour and energy to the achievement of these (see box 3.1).

Evidence linking engagement to performance

Engagement shows a clear, significant correlation with performance and customer satisfaction, according to research primarily conducted in the private sector (see Bakker, 2011; MacLeod and Clarke, 2011). There are two primary approaches to studying engagement. One approach focuses on the organisational level of analysis; this has been developed and promoted primarily by private consulting firms (e.g. Gallup, Kenexa, Aeon Hewitt, the Hay Group and Towers Watson). Another approach, generally referred to as *work engagement*, has been developed primarily in the academic sphere and focuses on the engagement of individual employees with their work.

The organisational stream has produced various studies linking engagement indicators in employee surveys with organisational performance. Harter, Schmidt and Hayes (2002) conducted a meta-analysis of data collected by the Gallup Organisation (36 companies and 7 939 business units) and found that engagement is related to business-unit performance and especially to customer satisfaction measures. Influenced by this line of research, a UK initiative, *Engage for Success*, was established to explore the implications of what appeared to be low levels of engagement in the United Kingdom across all business sectors. This "engagement deficit", it is argued, has significant implications for overall workforce productivity in the private and public sectors. The initiative cites the following evidence linking engagement to profit, customer satisfaction, productivity and innovation (Rayton et al., 2012):

- **Profit**: Private consultancy firms show a strong link between their measures of employee engagement and firm profitability. Gallop, Aeon Hewitt, Kenexa, the Hay Group and Towers Watson are among the private firms that have looked at large samples of surveyed employees, often in multiple countries and consistently shown that companies that score within the highest quartile for employee engagement perform far better on a range of financial indicators including total net income, one-year operating margins, revenue growth, and shareholder value.
- **Customer satisfaction**: A range of private studies claim a strong link between engaged front-line customer-facing staff and customer indicators such as satisfaction, loyalty and advocacy (customers who actively promote a company to their contacts). In the back-office, high engagement was associated with better production, fewer processing errors, and thereby better client outcomes. The link between engagement and client impact is also found in the public sector. For example, one study shows that 78% of highly engaged public sector employees say they are able to make an impact on public service delivery, while only 29% of disengaged employees feel the same way. Data from the UK National Health Service suggest links between engagement, patient satisfaction, and even patient mortality.
- **Productivity**: Research indicates strong links between employee engagement and behaviours associated with a more productive workforce. Engaged employees perform their tasks better, more efficiently and with fewer errors. Aside from working productively, engagement is also highly correlated with higher employee retention and well-being. Research by some private consultancy firms suggests that disengaged employees can be up to four times more likely to leave an organisation. Research also shows that engaged employees show higher levels of well-being all around, experience less work-related stress, and are less often absent.
- **Innovation**: Data and research correlate high engagement scores with innovation. Engaged employees show more personal initiative and innovative work behaviour. They tend to be more involved and socially connected to their work, which allows more opportunity to contribute to improvement and innovation. Gallup data indicate that 59% of engaged employees said that their job brings out their most creative ideas, against only 3% of disengaged employees.

Academics studying engagement have raised concerns regarding the ability to verify evidence presented by private consultancy firms due to the proprietary nature of their data. Although many of the links claimed by consultancies may be true, some suggest that their approach falls short of providing actionable insights. Dr David Guest (2014) points out a lack of clarity on what is meant by the term and what is being measured, which in turn raises questions regarding the quality of evidence. Without clear causation and antecedents, these studies do not provide an organisation with a clear roadmap to enhance engagement. This may, in part, be due to the organisational focus of the studies, which may fail to take into consideration the individual employee's interests.

Instead, Dr Guest and others point to a stream of research on work engagement that transparently addresses many of the criticisms explored above. With this research, analysis is conducted at the individual level, and linked to individual work behaviours. Some key findings of the research are:

- Work engagement is proven to be one the best predictors of individual task performance and organisational citizenship behaviour (loosely defined as voluntary activities that go beyond the tasks required in a work contract and that support organisational effectiveness) (Rich et al 2010).
- Guest (2014) references a summary by Peccei who shows significant links between work engagement and task performance, contextual performance, health, and intention to quit.
- Bakker (2009) discusses four reasons that link engagement with better employee performance: "Engaged employees: 1) often experience positive emotions, including happiness, joy, and enthusiasm; 2) experience better psychological and physical health; 3) create their own job and personal resources (e.g., support from others); and 4) transfer their engagement to others."

The construct of work engagement enables researchers to more clearly define its antecedents and drivers. These include the following:

- Rich et al (2010) found that high levels of value congruence (employee-organisation fit), perceived organisational support, and core self-evaluations were significant determinants of employee engagement.
- Bakker (2009) looks at job resources and personal resources as sources of engagement. Job resources refer to physical, social and organisational factors that support job performance. These may include physical surroundings, workplace culture and/or opportunities for learning and development. Personal resources refer to attributes of employees themselves, such as optimism, resilience and self-efficacy.
- Guest (2014) summarises work by Peccei who finds that job variety, work-role fit, task significance and self-efficacy to be the strongest antecedents of work engagement.

Engaged workers who enjoy their work and identify with their employer also have a role to play in winning back lost trust in public administration. Building on the established correlation between employee engagement and customer satisfaction, Heintzman and Marson (2005) explore the existence of a public sector value chain that links engaged employees (defined in their research as job satisfaction and organisational commitment) to customer satisfaction, thereby increasing citizen trust and confidence in government services. This study shows that investing in human capital and engagement can have a direct outcome on citizen perceptions and trust in government. The German Employment Agency (BA) came to similar conclusions upon analysis of its employee engagement data (see Box 3.2).

Figure 3.1. Public sector value chain: Links between engagement, citizen satisfaction and trust

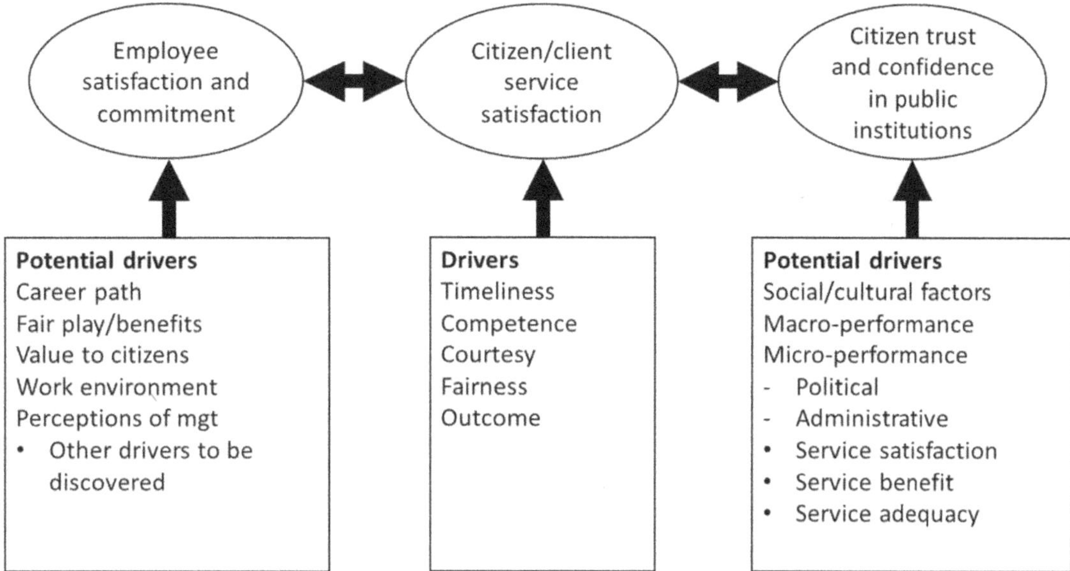

Source: Adapted from Heintzman, R. and B. Marson (2005), "People, service, trust: is there a public sector service value chain?", *International Review of Administrative Sciences*, Vol. 71, No. 4, pp.549–575, http://ras.sagepub.com/content/71/4/549.

Box 3.2. Engagement research in Germany

A representative study done in 314 companies on behalf of the German Federal Ministry of Labour showed a clear relationship between organisational culture, quality of work, employee engagement and business success. The study presented a significant relationship between employee engagement and financial success, and levels of sickness absence in the companies. The positive correlation between engagement and performance is due to: the person's positive and optimistic attitude, which boosts creativity and solution orientation; good health, which allows the person to mobilise all of their energy; the active seeking of feedback and support; and the positive infection and inspiration of others in their environment (Bakker, Demerouti & Sanz-Vergel, 2014).

Research results from BA, which followed the second round of the engagement index, confirm the empirical findings and show the impact of employee engagement and client satisfaction measured at BA on an annual base (see Figure 3.2).

Figure 3.2. Path analyses of the relationship between engagement and client satisfaction

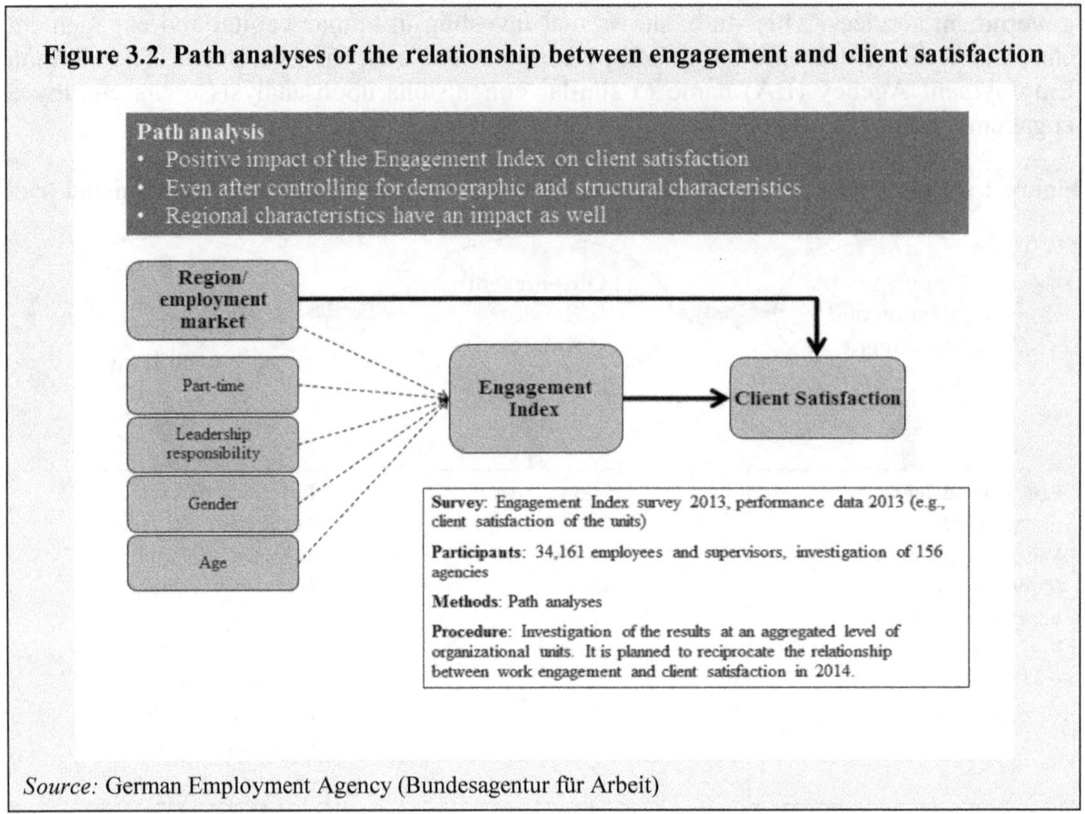

Source: German Employment Agency (Bundesagentur für Arbeit)

Managing engagement in OECD countries: An evidence-based approach to benchmark performance

Evidence presented in Chapter 2 on HRM cost reduction measures between 2008 and 2013 indicates potential reductions in work engagement resulting from significant HRM cost cutting measures in most OECD countries. These measures have often resulted in greater job intensity and work-related stress, and lower trust in leadership, job satisfaction, and workplace commitment. These concepts are significantly related to employee engagement.

Many countries are, therefore, trying to actively manage employee engagement. This is usually based on a process of measurement through employee surveys, which enable public organisations to benchmark their results, identify areas of high and low engagement, and take appropriate action. Well-designed employee surveys enable an understanding not only of relative levels of engagement across and within organisations, but also the factors that drive low or high engagement, and thereby the levers available to management to address and improve engagement.

This can be a particularly powerful tool when, for example, two similar work units display very different levels of engagement. The UK survey, for example, shows a high range of employee survey results among different units within the same ministry or agency. Analysis of the 2013 results suggests that engagement scores could be significantly improved by encouraging learning from the high performers within individual ministries and agencies (UK Cabinet Office, 2013).

Interest in the potential of employee surveys is growing across OECD central governments as they begin to understand the potential that these surveys can have in developing an evidence base that can be used to gauge performance, benchmark organisations and target management actions. A recent survey by the OECD (summarised in Table 2.1 below) shows that 18 countries conduct centralised surveys across the full central public administration (CPA) at regular intervals. Conversely, only five countries report not using employee surveys at all. Fifteen OECD countries run their surveys annually, while five run theirs every two years. Employee surveys are a current area of reform activity in 10 OECD countries (including a number of countries that indicate not yet using the instrument), and an area of significant reform discussion in an additional 16 countries.

Table 3.1. The use and frequency of employee surveys in OECD civil services (2016)

	Employee survey data							
	Employee surveys are conducted...				**Frequency**			
	across the central public administration	by administrative sectors	by each ministry/agency	Not conducted	On an as-needed basis	Every year	Every 2 years	More seldom than every two years
Australia	●	○	●	○	●	●	○	○
Austria	●	○	○	○	○	○	○	●
Belgium	○	○	●	○	●	○	●	○
Canada	●	○	●	○	●	○	○	●
Chile	●	●	●	○	●	●	○	●
Czech Republic	●	○	●	○	○	●	○	○
Denmark	0	○	●	○	○	●	○	○
Estonia	●	○	●	○	●	●	●	●
Finland	●	○	●	○	○	●	○	○
France	●	●	●	○	○	○	○	●
Germany	○	○	●	○	●	○	○	○
Greece	○	○	○	●	○	○	○	○
Hungary	○	○	○	●	○	○	○	○
Iceland	●	○	●	○	●	●	○	○
Ireland	●	○	○	○	○	●	○	○
Israel	●	○	○	○	○	●	○	○
Italy	○	○	●	○	○	○	○	●
Japan	○	○	○	●	○	○	○	○
Korea	●	○	○	○	○	○	○	●
Luxembourg	○	○	○	●	○	○	○	○
Mexico	●	●	○	○	○	●	○	○
Netherlands	○	●	●	○	○	○	●	●
New Zealand	○	○	●	○	●	○	○	○
Norway	●	○	○	○	○	○	○	●
Poland	○	○	●	○	●	○	○	○
Portugal	●	○	○	○	○	○	●	○
Slovak Republic	○	●	○	○	●	○	○	○

Table 3.1. The use and frequency of employee surveys in OECD civil services (2016) *(continued)*

	Employee survey data							
	Employee surveys are conducted...				Frequency			
	across the central public administration	by administrative sectors	by each ministry/agency	Not conducted	On an as-needed basis	Every year	Every 2 years	More seldom than every two years
Slovenia	○	○	●	○	○	●	○	○
Spain	○	○	○	●	○	○	○	○
Sweden	○	○	●	○	○	○	●	○
Switzerland	●	○	○	○	○	●	○	●
Turkey	○	●	●	○	●	●	○	○
United Kingdom	●	○	○	○	○	●	○	○
United States	●	●	●	○	○	●	○	○
Lithuania	○	○	○	○	○	○	○	○
Latvia	●	○	○	○	○	○	●	○
Colombia	●	○	●	○	●	●	●	○
Costa Rica	○	○	○	●	○	○	○	○
Flanders	●	○	○	○	○	○	●	○
● Yes	21	7	20	6	12	16	8	10
○ No	17	32	19	33	27	23	31	29

Source: OECD (2016), *Survey on Strategic Human Resources Management in Central/Federal Governments of OECD Countries*, OECD, Paris.

While the use of employee surveys is a clear trend in OECD countries, and is contributing to a more data-driven and individualised HRM, the focus of employee surveys varies significantly across countries. Not all employee surveys are currently designed to measure engagement and its drivers, although a majority (21 countries) appear to address the concept in some form.

Figure 3.3. Focus of employee surveys in OECD countries (number of countries) (2016)

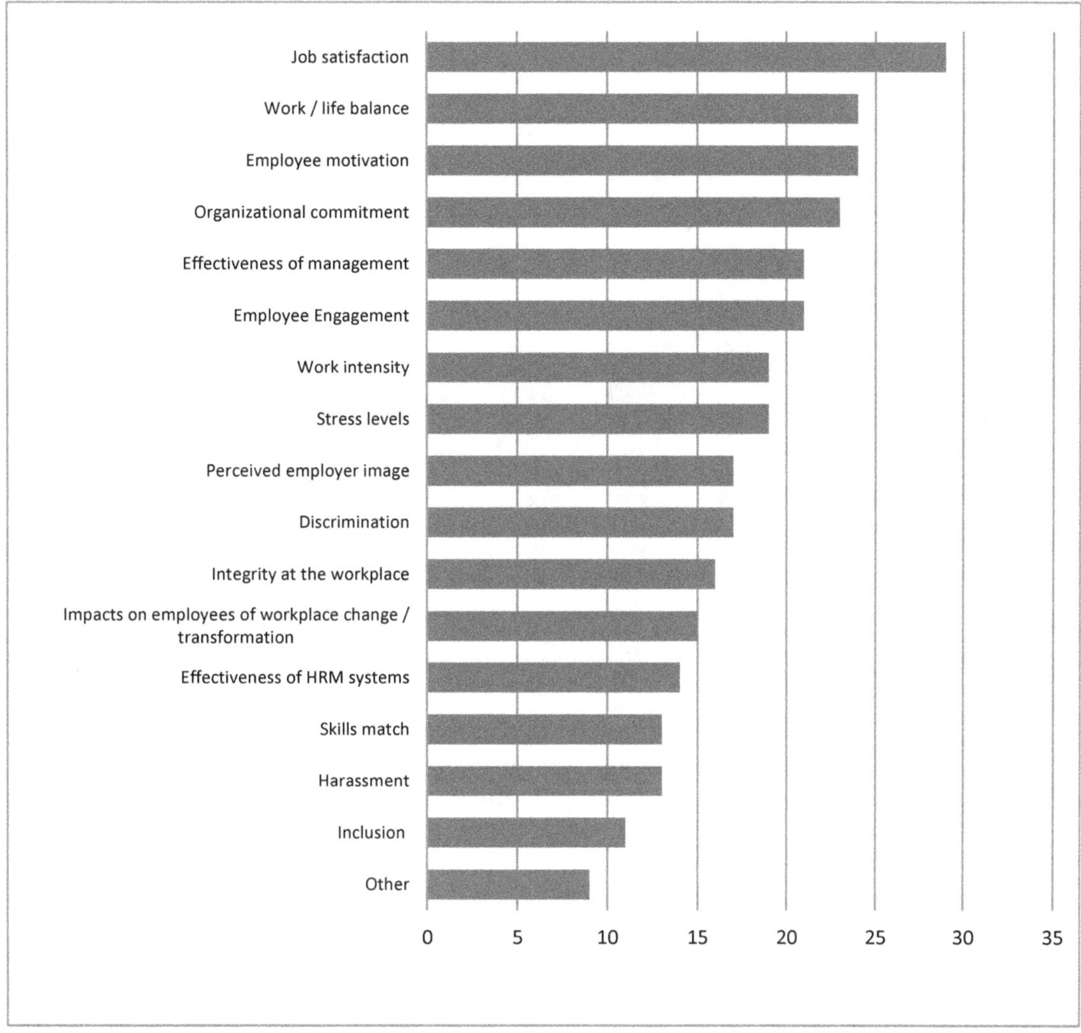

Source: OECD (2016), *Survey on Strategic Human Resources Management in Central/Federal Governments of OECD Countries*, OECD, Paris.

Measuring employee engagement through employee surveys will not, in itself, contribute to improving employee engagement levels if nothing is done with the results. Of the countries that collect regular data from employee surveys, almost all report results to senior level management; many (18 countries) report results to the political level; while fewer (16 countries) make the results available to the public. Significantly fewer countries systematically use the data for decision making. For example, only a minority of countries report developing dashboards for management decision making, or integrating the data into the workforce planning cycle. This suggests a clear and ongoing need to explore opportunities to collect the data and interpret, present and use it in a way that drives improvement.

Figure 3.4. The use of employee survey data in OECD countries (number of countries) (2016)

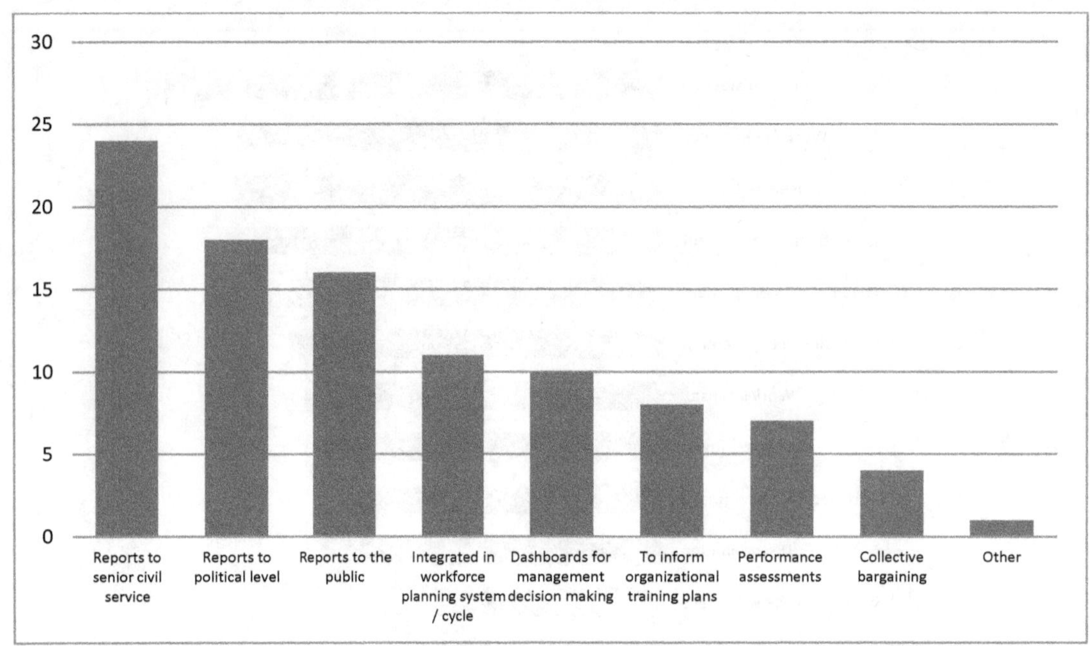

Source: OECD (2016), *Survey on Strategic Human Resources Management in Central/Federal Governments of OECD Countries*, OECD, Paris.

The OECD has begun collecting and analysing various employee engagement approaches of member countries. Table 2.2 illustrates the similarities and differences between the approaches collected.

Table 3.2. Case studies of employee engagement approaches: Similarities and variations

Similarities	Variations
• Empirical methodology based on conducting online surveys. • Survey conducted on a regular basis, mainly annual. • Overall goal: fostering performance and strengthening leadership and collaboration. • Strengthening responsibility and capacity at management level for a follow-up process. • Managing a diverse workforce and using the results for further research connected to socio-demographic data.	• Degree to which engagement is in the survey's focus. • Degree to which the engagement concept is embedded in an overall governmental and HRM strategy. • Additional goals: working conditions well-being, culture, diversity, employer branding. • Different degree to which follow-up process is tracked. • Different approaches to stakeholder participation in developing and designing the survey. • Different evaluation levels: top management (only) versus up to middle management. • Relevance of engagement as a topic in the qualification of supervisors and leadership training. • Inclusion in target management and performance related pay. • Degree of how data are used to evaluate and improve policy-making processes/controlling.

Country case studies highlight a range of data-driven, evidence-based approaches for identifying and addressing employee engagement. While approaches differ in many ways, there is a common goal: to improve the culture of leadership and collaboration in order to perform better on the individual and organisational level, and to be attractive and competitive employers.

The case studies collected show how some OECD countries are using survey results to inform HRM and leadership approaches with a view to improving employee engagement over the medium term, and thereby ensuring better organisational outcomes.

Measuring engagement in the US and UK civil services, and in the German Employment Agency

Both the United States and the United Kingdom conduct extensive annual surveys of their entire federal/national civil service workforce, with a view to measuring and comparing employee engagement and staff perceptions. In Germany, BA presents a third model of engagement in action within a single large public agency. This section will look at these cases in more detail to illustrate three ways the engagement concept is incorporated into public HRM.

In the United States, engagement was made a core component of President Obama's management agenda to "innovate by unlocking the full potential of the workforce we have today and build the workforce we need for tomorrow". Central to this mission is the Office of Personnel Management's (OPM) Federal Employee Viewpoint Survey (FEVS), "a tool to measure employees' perceptions of whether, and to what extent, conditions characterising successful organisations are present in their agencies" (www.fedview.opm.gov/). In 2015, 421 748 employees from 82 agencies responded to the survey. Analysis of the data conducted by OPM enables a breakdown and comparison across the 82 agencies (grouped by size), as well as down to 28 000 work units with a minimum of 10 respondents. Managers can access the results through an online portal (unlocktalent.org), which enables them to analyse the scores of their unit and compare them to other units within their organisation.

OPM defines employee engagement as a sense of purpose, "evident from [the employee's] display of dedication, persistence and effort in their work and overall commitment to their organisation and its mission" (OPM, 2015: 6). The FEVS engagement index measures employee perceptions of their organisation's leadership, the quality of their relationship with their supervisor, and the employee's intrinsic work experience (see Box 2.4).

The UK's civil service people survey (UK Cabinet Office, 2013) is one of the largest employee attitudes surveys carried out in the United Kingdom each year. More than 400 000 civil servants are invited to participate, and in 2015, the survey received 279 653 responses from employees in 96 organisations, an overall response rate of around 65%. The main form of reporting is through the organisational hierarchy: teams with at least 10 respondents are able to get a report of their scores, resulting in around 10 000 reports produced each year, so that groups can be benchmarked and action taken at the right level to produce positive improvement. In addition to the team-level benchmarking, the size of the dataset allows for cross-governmental analysis and reporting (see Box 2.3).

As with the United States, the United Kingdom also measures employee engagement as a key performance indicator, and describes it as, "a workplace approach designed to ensure that employees are committed to their organisation's goals and values, motivated to contribute to organisational success, and are able at the same time to enhance their own sense of well-being." While the description differs from that of the United States, they both seek to align effort and motivation to organisational outcomes. Significant differences also exist between US and UK measurements. While the US index includes 15 questions, the UK index includes only 5 key questions in the survey related to personal/emotional indicators of an employee's relationship to their work and their workplace: pride, advocacy, attachment, inspiration and motivation. The UK survey also assesses employees' perceptions of their work, their supervisor and their organisations' leadership, but these are analysed separately as drivers of engagement, along with others, and are therefore not included in the engagement index.

Box 3.3. UK civil service people survey: Cross governmental analysis

Prior to the single survey approach, different departments and agencies ran their own surveys. However, the single survey approach gives departments greater abilities to benchmark against each other through the use of a standardised questionnaire. Although a collaborative effort between departments and agencies, the single survey approach is co-ordinated by the Cabinet Office, which is also responsible for analysis and reporting on cross-government results.

The annual cycle of the single survey provides the Cabinet Secretary and the other permanent secretaries[1] to have a data-driven discussion on the way in which the civil service is managed and led. While permanent secretaries remain responsible for actions in their own department and its agencies, analysis of the cross-government results, including departmental comparisons, is discussed at the Civil Service Board to identify common priorities across the civil service.

Another form of cross-government analysis is the analysis provided to communities of professionals in government (e.g. economists, statisticians, lawyers, HRM, finance professionals). Before the single survey approach, each cross-government professional community conducted their own survey to gauge sentiments within their community. Instead, the People Survey includes a question asking respondents their occupation, and the 200+ responses available are combined into 34 major occupational groups for analysis. Analysis of these occupational results is provided to the co-ordination teams for the professions. Alongside the overall results for the profession, the analysis often includes breakdowns of the profession's results by other demographics, such as grade and department.

Note: [1]A Permanent Secretary is the most senior official in a government department and is responsible for all officials working in their department. The Cabinet Secretary is the most senior civil servant in the United Kingdom, they are responsible to the Prime Minister for the management of the civil service. Cabinet Secretaries chair the Civil Service Board, which sets the overall strategy for the management of the civil service.

Source: UK Cabinet Office (2013), *Civil Service People Survey*, Cabinet Office, London, http://webarchive.nationalarchives.gov.uk/20140305122816/http://resources.civilservice.gov.uk/wp-content/uploads/2014/02/csps2013_summary_of_findings.pdf.

BA provides another example of a public agency using an engagement index as a leadership tool to support organisational development. It is Germany's largest federal agency, with about 98 000 employees nationwide located in more than 1 000 agencies and branch offices. Germany does not have a national engagement survey comparable to the UK or US models. Thus, BA developed a tailor-made engagement index for its organisation: The engagement index of the BA is central to HRM and business strategy, including the BA 2020 strategy, which has a stated business goal to "motivate employees and recognise and tap potentials", in order to promote customer satisfaction (also being measured) of a service-oriented public administration. The engagement index is included in the goal management of the BA as an employee/resource oriented goal and is connected with performance related payment for top Executives.

For BA, employee engagement consists of goal-oriented behaviours including the willingness to perform and the ability to perform. It also concerns the continuous improvement of leadership and collaboration, including the psychological contract (explained below) and the design of working relationships. The BA engagement index is made up of 19 questions with 5 dimensions: 1) willingness to strive; 2) identification; 3) psychological contract; 4) workability; and 5) communication. Additional questions are asked regarding enablers of engagement: work organisation, colleagues, leadership, qualification, appreciation.

Box 3.4. Engagement indices in the United States, the United Kingdom and Germany's Employment Agency (BA)

United States: focus on management support	
Leaders Lead	• In my organisation, senior leaders generate high levels of motivation and commitment in the workforce. • My organisation`s senior leaders maintain high standards of honesty and integrity. • Managers communicate the goals and priorities of the organisation. • Overall, how good a job do you feel is being done by the manager directly above your immediate supervisor? • I have a high level of respect for my organisation`s senior leaders.
Supervisors	• Supervisors in my work unit support employee development. • My supervisor listens to what I have to say. • My supervisor treats me with respect. • I have trust and confidence in my supervisor. • Overall, how good a job do you feel is being done by your immediate supervisor?
Intrinsic work motivation	• I feel encouraged to come up with new and better ways of doing things. • My work gives me a feeling of personal accomplishment. • I know what is expected of me on the job. • My talents are used well in the workplace. • I know how my work relates to the agency's goals and priorities.
United Kingdom: focus on organisational commitment	
Pride	• I am proud when I tell others I am part of [my organisation] *Rationale: An engaged employee feels proud to be associated with their organisation, by feeling part of it rather than just "working for" it.*
Advocacy	• I would recommend [my organisation] as a great place to work *Rationale: An engaged employee will be an advocate of their organisation and the way it works.*
Attachment	• I feel a strong personal attachment to [my organisation] *Rationale: An engaged employee has a strong, and emotional, sense of belonging to their organisation.*
Inspiration	• [My organisation] inspires me to do the best in my job *Rationale: An engaged employee will contribute their best, and it is important that their organisation plays a role in inspiring this.*
Motivation	• [My organisation] motivates me to help it achieve its objectives *Rationale: An engaged employee is committed to ensuring their organisation is successful in what it sets out to do.*

Box 3.4. Engagement indices in the United States, the United Kingdom and Germany's Employment Agency (BA) *(continued)*

BA: focus on teams, values and goal-oriented behaviour	
Willingness to strive	• I work on my tasks persistently and in a goal-oriented way. • I have a strong drive to achieve work results of a high quality. • My colleagues can rely on my support even under difficult circumstances. • I use my competencies in order to perform my job well. • I am willing to do my best to achieve the team goals.
Identification	• I identify with the mission of the BA. • I support changes at the BA as far as possible. • I align my daily work towards the goals of my agency. • If I had the choice once more today, I would choose the BA as an employer again.
Psychological contract	• At work I have the possibility to do what I can do best. • I can adequately bring in my expectations and ideas to my employment relationship. • My work is more than just a job to me (e.g., contribution to common welfare).
Workability	• Overall, I can manage my workload (amount and quality) well. • I am convinced that I can handle my job requirements permanently. • I actively contribute to my work and private obligations being compatible.
Communication	• I actively participate in meetings. • In everyday working life I actively contribute to enthusing my colleagues for ideas. • I actively contribute to successful information exchange within the team. • I encourage colleagues to support team goals with all their might.

A comparison of these three indices suggests a great deal of variation in the definition and measurement of engagement. What is common and important is that each of the examples presents an empirically sound methodology to assess employees' perceptions of their work and working environment, with a view to improving the factors that limit an employee's abilities to achieve their full potential. Regardless of the number of questions in the index, or the name of the concept (engagement, commitment, etc.), the power of the tool is in its ability to assess and benchmark using empirical evidence focused on employee perceptions. Unlike traditional performance assessment approaches, which focus on incentivising performance at the individual level, these approaches are designed to assess the work, the environment and the management qualities in order to promote learning, collaboration and better leadership.

Although it is not the goal of the OECD to judge one index's value over another, some countries have expressed an interest in building a common set of questions that could provide international comparability, so that civil services as a whole can better understand how they compare and differ in relation to their international peers. This work is currently being explored by the OECD's Public Governance Committee.

Drivers of employee engagement: From analysis to action

Measurement alone is rarely enough to produce change. Beyond the engagement indices, each of the surveys contains many additional questions. Through statistical analysis, particular questions are identified as drivers of the engagement scores, which suggest paths for action to improve engagement. Improving the area indicated by the driver (e.g. leadership, supervision, or training and development opportunities) should result in improving engagement.

In the United States, The Government Accountability Office (GAO) suggests that the strongest drivers of the US employee engagement index are constructive performance conversations, career development and training, work-life balance, inclusive work environments, employee involvement, and communication from management.

In 2014, each agency in the United States was asked to designate one senior official responsible for improving employee engagement. These officials work with the OPM to understand their agency's results, including benchmarks and drivers. Agencies are encouraged to use the index score as a general indicator of progress, and are provided with detailed breakdowns in order to pinpoint specific drivers that may underperform. This enables a tailored and targeted intervention.

The OPM also makes an effort to highlight organisations with the most impressive scores on the Federal Employee Viewpoint Survey (FEVS) and those with the greatest improvements over the year.[1] In 2016, the top increase in scores was achieved by the US Department of Energy, which took a multi-pronged approach to directly addressing employee engagement (see Box 2.5).

Box 3.5. Strengthening employee engagement at the US Department of Energy

The US Department of Energy's (DOE) scores on the Federal Employee Viewpoint Survey (FEVS) were in significant decline from 2011 to 2014. In December 2014, the Administration issued a memorandum providing direction and guidance that directed agencies to strengthen employee engagement and organisational performance.[1] DOE took on this challenge using a multi-pronged approach to strengthen employee engagement.

Strategies and actions taken to address low engagement scores:

1. **Leaders set clear goals and review progress**: The Secretary and DOE senior leaders visibly communicated their commitment, expectations, and goals for strengthening employee engagement. For instance, leaders held programme-level all-hands meetings with employees within 60 days of the Secretary's Town Hall. Leaders demonstrated commitment to employee engagement goals by interacting regularly with employees in a variety of ways. Information obtained was incorporated into agency and program action plans. This was a shift from the previous top-down only approach which led to positive results. In addition, the Office of the Chief Human Capital Officer (CHCO) met with programmes to discuss successes and challenges in employee engagement, and reported progress regularly to the Secretary and Deputy Secretary.
2. **Senior Executive Service (SES) members and managers are supported and held accountable for improvement**: DOE appointed Senior Accountable Officials (SAO) to implement Administration requirements. In 2016, all SES performance plans included a measurable element, along with training and consultations, related to action planning and/or results to improve employee engagement.
3. **FEVS data is disseminated and organised for action**: DOE created a first-of-its-kind Organisational Management Report (OMR) and analysis tool to support data interpretation and action planning. In 2016, FEVS results were disseminated for 520 work units down to seven organisational levels across the Department, and in support of transparency, all reports will be made available to employees.

Box 3.5. Strengthening employee engagement at the US Department of Energy *(continued)*

4. **Increased adoption of employee-driven and evidence-based practices**: The CHCO led and managed collaborations with the DOE Labor Management Forum and DOE Program Offices to share successful practices and common engagement challenges, and implement employee-led recommendations. In addition, DOE Workplace Improvement Networks (WIN) were launched in Headquarters and Field Offices to expand the practice of employee-led workplace improvement at local levels throughout the Department.

Measurable impact:

In 2016, DOE led all "Large Agencies" (10,000 to 74,999 federal employees) for increases in overall Engagement and all three engagement sub factors, as well as for increases in overall Inclusion and all five Habits of Inclusion. In addition, DOE's Workplace Improvement Networks have produced visible employee-driven improvements in facilities and programs throughout the Department.

Note: [1] https://www.whitehouse.gov/sites/default/files/omb/memoranda/2015/m-15-04.pdf

Source: Information provided by the US PEM Delegate.

The US Department of Labour (DOL) moved from being second to last in the large agency category in the Best Places to Work in the Federal Government in 2013, to the top ten for 2014 and 2015. The DOL has also been the most improved large agency two years in a row. This significant accomplishment is described in more detail in Box 2.6.

Box 3.6. Improving engagement at the US Department of Labour

The US Department Of Labour's (DOL) FEVS results, prior to Secretary Perez's arrival, were consistently low. At the time, there was little attention being paid by Departmental leaders to FEVS results, and a great deal of resistance to the survey had built over the years. This lack of leadership attention with workforce engagement matters was offset with an increased focus on measures and accountability. The combined effect was a lower employee response rate of less than 50%.

Strategies and actions taken to address low engagement scores:

Secretary Perez, leadership, HRM and unions came together to discuss improvement. Secretary Perez's appointment in July 2013 marked the beginning of a renewed focus on FEVS and, in particular, a focus on improving workforce engagement. DOL engaged in extensive data collection and analysis, with the involvement of the Chief Evaluation Officer and the Office of the Assistant Secretary for Administration and Management (OASAM) leaders. Senior level management meetings were held to set expectations regarding improved employee engagement through improving communications, securing employee and union input in improvement strategies, and taking actions to address employee concerns and act on their suggestions. The Secretary conducted many town hall meetings, and listening sessions were conducted in most DOL offices across the country. A suggestion box was implemented and IDEAMILL, an ideation platform, was created. All of these strategies aimed to secure employee suggestions for improvement.

Box 3.6. Improving engagement at the US Department of Labour *(continued)*

DOL formed a small group of senior management to focus on FEVS efforts, with members across senior management, including: the Deputy Chief of Staff, others from the Secretary's office, and the office of the Chief Human Capital Officer. This group interviewed other agencies to secure ideas. Three areas of focus were identified, based on the data analysis and input: leadership, training and innovation. Customised agency action plan templates were created to track progress and articulate plans. The group meets weekly to manage initiatives and communications.

Secretary Perez met with DOL's three union presidents and asked for their suggestions on improving FEVS scores, and he has continued to meet with union leadership periodically to secure feedback and input. DOL unions have been very supportive of the Secretary's efforts to improve engagement and create a more flexible work environment.

Results of the strategy:

The efforts have resulted in DOL being the most improved large agency two years in a row, moving from the second to last large agency in the Best Places to Work in the Federal Government in 2013 (see Box 2.16, to the top ten for 2014 and 2015. This achievement involved significant continuous and constant leadership attention.

Beyond survey scores, these efforts are building a new and better way of working at DOL:

- **Ongoing and frequent communication with staff**: This has taken place through town hall meetings, listening sessions and other forums. The level of management attention paid over the past three years has increased employee expectations for ongoing communication and a commitment to keep the workforce informed.
- **Improved relationships with the unions**: Not only have unions provided input on areas for improvement, they have been essential supporters of the Secretary's initiatives.
- **A more open and participative culture**: The DOL workforce has access to organisational results and agency action plans. Many DOL Agencies have instituted action planning at lower levels. Community of practice and other working groups have been created to focus on results and meaningful action planning. Overall union and workforce expectations of transparency have been increasing, and management concerns about information sharing have been decreasing.

Furthermore, the focus on employee engagement at DOL has led to the establishment of new programs like ROAD, a clearinghouse through which employees can find opportunities to detail to other agencies and sharpen their skills, and new workplace flexibilities that allow the DOL workforce to better balance their personal and professional lives.

Source: Information provided by the US PEM Delegate.

Statistical analysis over several years of UK People Survey scores consistently identifies leadership and effective change management as the strongest driver of employee engagement, followed by the nature of the work and an employee's relationship with their direct supervisor (see Figure 3.5 below).

As with the US approach, each manager of a team of at least 10 respondents receives a detailed report that summarises their team's scores. Scores are calculated for the engagement index, plus each of the nine survey themes. The dashboard compares these scores to those of their parent unit and their organisation, and to the average score for the civil service as a whole. The dashboard also tracks changes from previous years' surveys.

Additionally, teams are compared to the top quartile mark. Special analysis is conducted on questions related to well-being, discrimination and harassment, and employees' desires to remain or leave the organisation.

Figure 3.5. UK engagement model

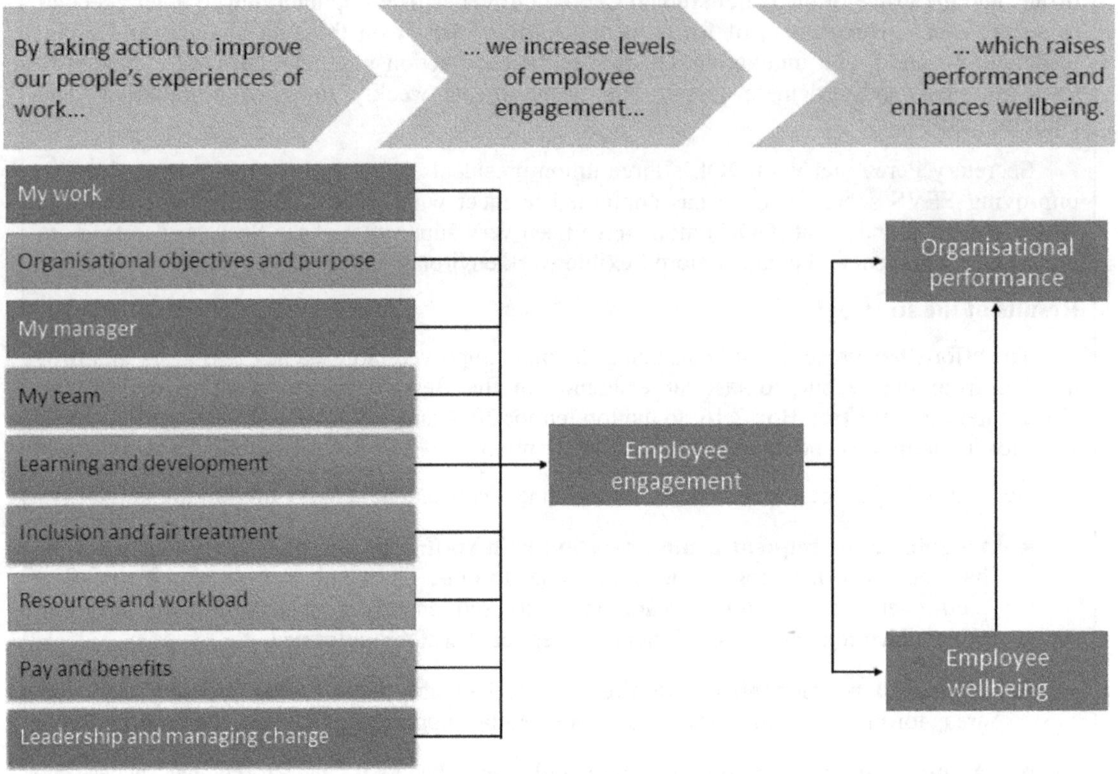

By taking action to improve our people's experiences of work...
... we increase levels of employee engagement...
... which raises performance and enhances wellbeing.

My work
Organisational objectives and purpose
My manager
My team
Learning and development
Inclusion and fair treatment
Resources and workload
Pay and benefits
Leadership and managing change
Employee engagement
Organisational performance
Employee wellbeing

Source: UK Cabinet Office (2013), *Civil Service People Survey*, Cabinet Office, London, http://webarchive.nationalarchives.gov.uk/20140305122816/http://resources.civilservice.gov.uk/wp-content/uploads/2014/02/csps2013_summary_of_findings.pdf.

Germany's BA has also conducted analysis on drivers, and has found that four main drivers can predict about 50% of the employee engagement score. These drivers are: work organisation, support by supervisors, work environment, and psychological contract.

After the survey is conducted, results are shared transparently through an IT-supported Leadership Information Cockpit, which is provided by the controlling unit. BA then undertakes a structured follow-up process that involves workshops for managers to understand results, and support to develop a follow-up strategy. Workshops and support tend to focus on: dialogue-based local processes to bring local employees together with senior leaders to discuss results and concerns; opportunities for employees to contribute to continuous improvement; and discussions of well-being and health management. Furthermore, BA encourages the sharing of good engagement practices through regular network meetings and a planned "action database" with best practice examples.

Research based on the BA data over a period of three years shows that employee engagement promotes or increases customer satisfaction and has the potential to have a positive impact on other business aspects. This research reinforces the notion that promoting employee engagement, based on good employee oriented and inspirational leadership is an important driver to promote a healthy organisational environment. For a discussion of BA's use of engagement within the context of an HRM strategy, see Box 2.15.

Use of engagement indicators to manage diversity and inclusion

In addition to organisational benchmarking, the United States, the United Kingdom and Germany's BA conduct analysis to compare the experiences and views of specific demographic groups. This can contribute to a better understanding of the levels of inclusion of an increasingly diverse public sector workforce. It's worth noting, however, that while many OECD civil services appear to be using employee surveys to measure engagement; few indicate inclusion as a factor of assessment (see Figure 2.4 above). This may be a missed opportunity.

The US engagement index is analysed across five demographic categories: agency tenure, generation, disability status, supervisory status, and telework status. The report also looks at the experience of specific "mission critical occupations" (IT and cybersecurity, contract specialists, HRM specialists, auditors, economists) and STEM (science, technology, engineering and mathematics) occupations, which are particularly difficult to attract and retain. In this way, the employee survey can help to develop better employer branding strategies to attract the right workforce, and more targeted HRM strategies to retain them.

Box 3.7. Managing workforce diversity: Insights from the UK Civil Service People Survey

Cross-government analysis of the UK People Survey results can be produced for different diversity groups. This analysis sheds light on the different experiences of staff within the civil service. Overall, women are more engaged than men, as are ethnic minority staff when compared to their white colleagues. There is no strong difference in the views of lesbian gay and bisexual (LGB) staff compared to heterosexual staff, while disabled staff are substantially less engaged than those without a disability. These patterns have been relatively stable over the seven years that the survey has been running.

These global patterns mask some interesting insights when looking at further sub-groups. For example, although women overall are more engaged than men when they are compared at each grade level, there is no difference in the engagement levels of women in senior management roles compared to men at that level. Again, overall ethnic minority staff are more engaged than their white counterparts, but senior ethnic minority staff are less engaged than white senior managers. When looking at LGB staff, there is no difference between them and their heterosexual colleagues, regardless of grade, while at every grade level, disabled staff are significantly less engaged than their non-disabled colleagues. Overall, while LGB staff do not appear to report different levels of engagement and overall attitudes towards their work, they are 1.5 times more likely to report experiencing discrimination or bullying at work.

These variations are not uniform across departments and agencies. For example, when looking at the differences between non-disabled and disabled staff at the civil service level, there was a -9 percentage point difference in levels of employee engagement in 2014: the Department for Communities and Local Government had a -16 percentage point difference, while the National Crime Agency only had a -2 percentage point difference.

In early 2015, the civil service made publicly available extensive analyses of the People Survey for different diversity groups, in addition to their usual publication of civil service-level and department/agency-level results.

Box 3.7. Managing workforce diversity: Insights from the UK Civil Service People Survey *(continued)*

Analysis by diversity groups is not limited to quantitative analysis, but also includes analyses of the open-text comments question included in the survey. For example, open-text comments from disabled staff have been presented to the Permanent Secretary-led group on disability issues. These have helped provide richer details of the experiences of disabled staff than just the quantitative results on their own, and have helped to contextualise discussions about actions to be taken to improve the results.

Source: UK Cabinet Office (2013), *Civil Service People Survey*, Cabinet Office, London, http://webarchive.nationalarchives.gov.uk/20140305122816/http://resources.civilservice.gov.uk/wp-content/uploads/2014/02/csps2013_summary_of_findings.pdf.

The UK cabinet office also conducts analysis on key population groups in order to support its talent plan, which addresses diversity and inclusion for the UK civil service (see Box 3.7). For example, regarding the questions related to discrimination and harassment, the survey shows little difference between male and female respondents. Approximately 11% of white employees report experiencing discrimination at work, compared to 14% of respondents who identify as black and/or part of an ethnic minority group, and 17% of LGB respondents. However, respondents with a long-term limiting condition are 2.5 times more likely to report experiencing discrimination and/or bullying/harassment than their non-disabled colleagues. This kind of survey assessment can provide empirical evidence to inform diversity and inclusion strategies and planning, and can help to pinpoint areas that require more urgent attention.

The three cases presented above suggest different approaches to measuring engagement, assessing its drivers and using of the data to drive improvements. While the exact measurement of engagement differs across the three organisations, each has chosen to measure something that is more action-oriented than job satisfaction, and use it as a common performance indicator to benchmark organisations. Given the complexity of measuring performance in a comparative way across organisations with very different mandates, engagement surveys may present a rare opportunity to contribute to public sector performance measurement. The next challenge for these governments and others in the OECD who are actively addressing the topic (see Box 3.8) is to link employee survey data with other data sets related to both objective performance indicators and HRM data (e.g. retention rates, attractiveness, diversity indicators) to develop more complex models and insights to guide more effective management. The next section looks at what kind of management practices and HRM are required to support more engagement in public employees.

Box 3.8. Employee surveys and engagement in other OECD countries

Belgium Federal Government: Engagement is measured as part of a broader job satisfaction survey. The underlying framework defines nine topics (or "domains") that construct the canvas for the survey: 1) job content; 2) workplace; 3) recognition; 4) career; 5) responsibility/autonomy; 6) team and team manager; 7) interpersonal relationships; 8) communication; and 9) organisational culture. Engagement is not identified as one of the major topics; however, a number of questions that address the commitment of the employee are to be found in different domains. In some cases their focus is on organisational engagement, other questions address the subject of work engagement. Follow up on the survey is left to each organisation.

Box 3.8. Employee surveys and engagement in other OECD countries *(continued)*

Belgium Flanders Region: Engagement is not measured in a separate questionnaire, but relevant concepts are included in the satisfaction survey. Flanders also incorporates the concept of engagement into talent management and as a core component of a broader HRM strategy. The results of the general survey (overall data of the Flemish Public Service) are used to define general HRM policies and to assess the impact of those policies. The results of the organisations are used in their own HR management. The HRM agency (AgO) of public governance organises training sessions on how to interpret results and how to define an appropriate improvement plan that is integrated in the HR strategy of the organisation. Most define improvement projects in order to tackle the areas for improvement that are derived from the survey.

Estonia: In Estonian there is a term (*pühendumus*) that describes both engagement and commitment, it is defined as an "employee's attitude toward his/her employer that shapes his/her readiness to give the maximum" (TNS Emor, 2011). Estonia measures three components: emotional, behavioural and cognitive. The results of the study have initiated several training programmes and activities. For example, to increase the common understanding of strategically important issues, an annual conference for top civil servants is organised (regular since 2011); to increase the number of innovators among top civil servants, a joint programme with the Finnish public service called Government Needs Innovation, Innovation Needs Government was initiated; and talent management programmes within the public service for future top civil servants has been in place since 2008 in order to enhance co-operation in the public service

Ireland: In Ireland, the use of employee surveys supports the Irish Civil Service Renewal plan, which strives to deliver real improvements for the state and the people of Ireland. Staff engagement is defined as "the sense of energy, connection and fulfilment staff have with their work." Ireland ran its first civil-service wide employee survey in 2015. The results were published under four main themes: employee engagement, well-being, coping with change and commitment to the organisation. Analysis of the survey results suggests that staff are highly engaged and highly resilient, and feel positive about their work and their immediate working environment. Irish civil servants are less positive about their leaders and their organisations, and do not recognise a culture of involvement or innovation in the civil service. Another key perception is that their work is not fully valued by the public they serve. Comparing results between top leadership and junior grades reveals a number of differences, the most striking being that leaders are much more committed to the organisation, and perceive more organisational support and better opportunities for career development and mobility.

Australia: Australia's Public Service (APS) Employee Census provides fundamental data for the annual State of the APS report presented to the Australian Parliament by the Australian Public Service Commissioner. The 2016 APS employee census was administered to all available APS employees. This census approach provides a comprehensive view of the APS and ensures no eligible respondents are omitted from the survey sample. The census' content is designed to establish the views of APS employees on workplace issues such as leadership, learning and development and engagement. In 2016, the census ran from 9 May to 10 June 2016. Overall, 96 672 APS employees responded to the employee census, a response rate of 69%. The State of the Service Report 2015-16 is due to be tabled in parliament on 28 November 2016. Leading up to this, analysis and results are being published online at: http://stateoftheservice.apsc.gov.au/. Australia also makes the datasets available through its online data portal, which is free of charge at: https://data.gov.au/dataset/aps-employee-census-2016.

Sources: Belgium, Estonia, Ireland: information submitted to the OECD secretariat. Australia: adapted from Australian Government (2016), Dataset on employee census, https://data.gov.au/dataset/aps-employee-census-2016, (accessed October 2016).

Promoting employee engagement through leadership and the psychological contract

As the examples highlighted in the previous section suggest, engagement is not a stable property; rather, it refers to a variable state exhibited by a person. There are, therefore, various approaches to promoting engagement, all with the end goal of enabling and supporting employees to participate in work and to align their own actions with the organisation's goals. In the work context, the first considerations are leadership and the relationship between managers and their employees. This also requires analysis of the design of the job's framework conditions. This section will look at leadership and management, while the next section will look more broadly at the framework conditions implied.

Box 3.9. Leadership driving employee engagement: correlations from select OECD countries

Despite the differences in measuring employee engagement, studies conducted at the national level and based on employee surveys indicate that senior leadership is a key driver of employee engagement in the public service. For example:

- In **Australia**: Based on the Autralian Public Service (APS) employee census, effective leadership is a key contributor to employee engagement. When asked whether they thought senior leaders in their organisation were sufficiently visible, employees who strongly agreed they were, showed substantially higher scores (double in some cases) on all components of employee engagement. Employees also value the opportunity to interact with their leaders in a meaningful way. In the APS, leaders who engage their employees in how to deal with the challenges confronting their organisation have a very positive effect on engagement levels of their employees (APSC, 2013). http://www.apsc.gov.au/about-the-apsc/parliamentary/state-of-the-service/2011-12-sosr/04-employee-engagement.
- In **Canada**: Employees who held positive opinions of senior management tended to express higher levels of engagement, particularly satisfaction with and commitment to their organization. The most notable differences in levels of engagement are between employees who have confidence in senior management and those who do not (Treasury Board of Canada, 2011). https://www.tbs-sct.gc.ca/pses-saff/2011/engage-mobil-eng.asp.
- In **Ireland**: Analysis based on the 2015 Civil Service Employee Engagement Survey revealed that the effectiveness of senior leadership was among the five key drivers of employee engagement along with employees' feeling that their job was meaningful, job skills match, competence and organisational support. (PER, 2016).
- In the **United Kingdom**: Statistical analysis over several years of the UK People Survey's scores consistently identifies leadership and effective change management as the strongest driver of employee engagement, followed by the nature of the work and an employee's relationship with their direct supervisor.
- In the **United States**: The analysis of the 2016 Employee Viewpoint Survey revealed that important drivers of engagement were related to the ability of senior leaders to 1) support fairness and protect employees from arbitrary actions, favoritism, political coercion, and reprisal; and 2) promote and support collaborative communication and teamwork in accomplishing goals and objectives and 3) support an effective recognition and reward system for good performance. (MPM, 2016) www.fedview.opm.gov/2016FILES/FEVS_Engagement_INFOGRAPHIC.pdf.

The psychological contract and the importance of good people managers

The psychological contract is a helpful concept to understand the impact of reforms, management and HRM on engagement and performance. The psychological contract includes mutual, subjective expectations on the part of the employee (e.g. appreciation, compatibility of private and professional life) and the employer (e.g. engagement, loyalty) that go beyond the legal contract of employment (Rousseau, 1995). It therefore addresses employees' needs and motives. How these non-legal expectations are perceived has a strong influence on engagement, commitment and motivation of employees. As part of the psychological contract, employees fulfil additional tasks if they have the feeling that the employer in turn will generally fulfil his/her obligations. A fulfilled psychological contract leads to consequences such as increased commitment, reduced psychological stress and increased job satisfaction. Reciprocity is the key norm that forms the psychological contract (Rousseau, 1995).

A helpful model and holistic approach that includes individual, organisational and HRM aspects is offered by Guest in Figure 2.6 (2004: 550).

Figure 3.6. Framework for applying the psychological contract to the employment relationship

Source: Guest, D. E. (2004), The Psychology of the Employment Relationship: An Analysis Based on the Psychological Contract. Applied Psychology, 53: 541–555. doi:10.1111/j.1464-0597.2004.00187.x.

Mutual expectations start during recruitment, where the future employee chooses an employer. Working conditions, payment and compensation, development opportunities, reconciliation of work and family, working time arrangements and corporate culture are attractive aspects of any employment offer. Once in the organisation, these "promises" should fit with the real and existing culture of the "employer of choice" from the employee's perspective.

Breaking the psychological contract has been shown to lead to frustration and organisational cynicism (Johnson and O'Leary-Kelly, 2003), disappointment and sick leave (Parzefall and Hakanen, 2010), and demotivation, disengagement and attrition of talent (Guest and Conway, 1997).

Change processes, such as those outlined in Chapter 2, generally break psychological contracts. In such situations, it must be assumed that not all mutual expectations or promises can (continue to) be fulfilled in an unchanged form. Examples of situations where psychological contracts might be broken include:

- New tasks are assigned as workforce reduction measures result in fewer people to do the work.
- The place of work has to be changed as part of workforce reallocation measures.
- Promotion opportunities are no longer available as the result of freezes or the reduction of management layers.
- Staff development measures or training are no longer carried out as promised.

The key issue concerns how psychological contracts for employees can be "managed". The appropriate measures to strengthen psychological contracts are to engage in dialogue with employees, and the development and use of dialogue-based management instruments in order to support leadership. These include regular performance discussions with employees. Performance feedback and staff development meetings should also be strongly geared towards the involvement and participation of employees. Personal life and career planning should be an active component that helps both sides to effectively plan for the future and to discover and correspondingly promote potential. These tools are not easy to use effectively.

This places expectations on the capacity of middle management – that is any manager who manages a team of people. Recent management research[2] shows that the quality of middle managers is fundamentally linked to organisational performance and employee engagement. However, managers promoted through the system are often unprepared to handle the complexities of people management, and require support in order to be prepared accordingly. Their development should include appropriate training measures based on a common leadership framework (leadership principles) and common values statements to be agreed upon between the manager and the employer. Middle managers should have access to support from coaches and management specialists, as well as a network of peers who can provide guidance based on personal experience.

The following measures show how the psychological contract can be strengthened from a leadership technique perspective (see Figure 3.7).

The management or fulfilment of mutual expectations between employee and employer is carried out by the direct line manager in the context of typical meetings, such as appraisal interviews, assessment interviews, discussions on agreeing objectives, and return and integration interviews. In the case of ongoing change processes, a considerable contribution to securing performance can be achieved if, in the context of a participatory approach, expectations and obligations are also actively worked out with employees during these meetings.

Figure 3.7. Leadership, the psychological contract and its effect on employee motivation and engagement

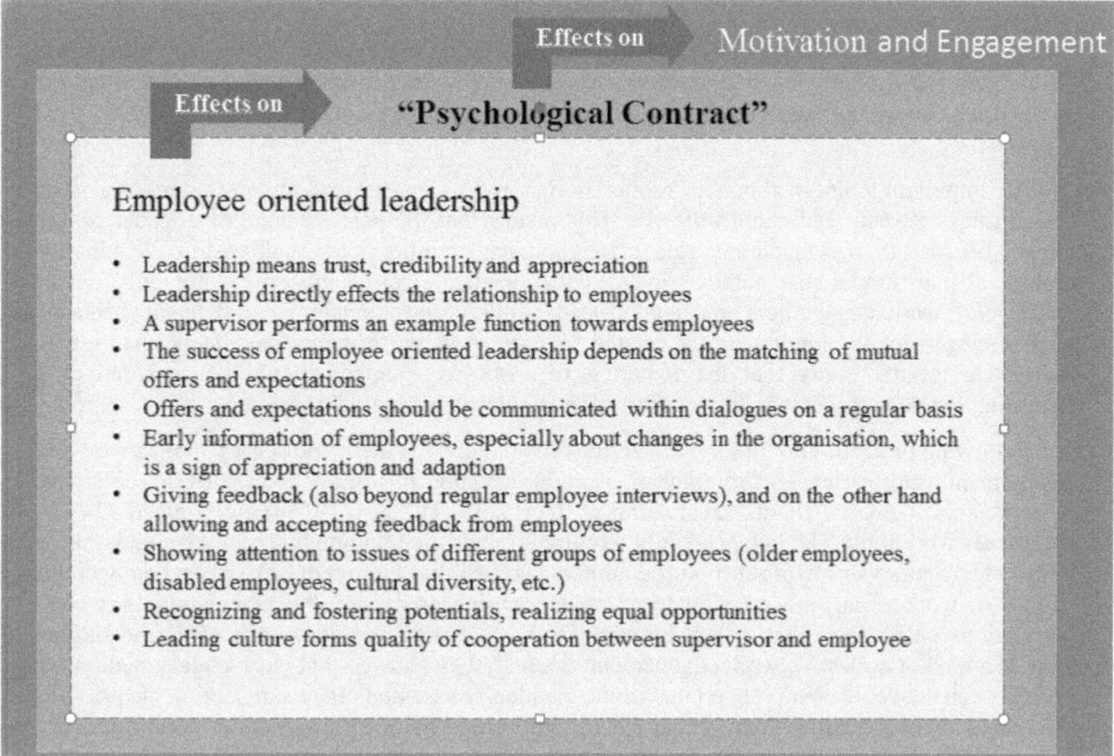

Source: Provided by the German Employment Agency.

The diversity of different expectations across different employees indicates the importance of developing a strategic framework for holistic management. The prerequisites for the individualised "management" of a psychological contract are appropriate service structures in the organisation, (which are explored in the next section) and consistent and sustained leadership support from those at the top of the organisational hierarchy.

Leadership style and employee engagement

The top leadership of an organisation has a significant influence on employees' levels of engagement. Recent research carried out by a team of German researchers (Gutermann et al., 2016a) in a public sector context suggests that engagement is transferred from leaders to their teams. This study, summarised in Box 3.10 below, provides empirical evidence that suggests engagement is contagious from the top down. Additional evidence shows that engagement also tends to be consistent among teams. Organisations with higher engagement overall were found to have better client satisfaction scores. This reinforces the link between engagement and client satisfaction, but adds the importance of engagement at the highest level.

Box 3.10. Empirical public sector study: Leadership matters

By surveying 511 employees working in 88 teams, and their respective leaders, researchers have shown that leaders play a key role in shaping employees' work engagement (Gutermann et al., 2016a). The study uncovered that leaders' own work engagement can transfer to their followers.

An important point within this model is that work engagement transfers due to a good relationship between leader and follower. This means that the positive state of a leader has an impact because of the mediating role of a good leader-subordinate-relationship. Within this multilevel path model, the authors revealed that leaders' work engagement not only boosts employees' work engagement via a good-leader-follower-relationship, but that subordinates' work engagement is simultaneously related to individual performance and their intention to leave. The results imply that the fostering of work engagement should be regarded as a cascading top down process within organisations (Gutermann et al., 2016a).

Following on from this finding, the authors investigated if there could be a "collective work engagement" at the level of organisations, and whether this may be related to collective performance, namely client satisfaction. Gutermann et al. (2016b) investigated 34 161 employees working in 156 independently working organisational units in a public administration body. The results were twofold: first the authors showed that there indeed exists a homogenous pattern of work engagement within teams and organisational units (by calculating intra-class correlation coefficients) that differs between teams and organisational units. This means that there is a kind of collective work engagement. Second, they showed that work engagement at the organisational level is positively related to independently assessed client satisfaction measures of the corresponding organisational units. This is important, as client satisfaction is an important organisational outcome, especially for firms in the service sector (Gutermann et. al., 2016b).

These results tie in with the findings of Harter, Schmidt and Hayes (2002), who showed among a diverse sample of different organisations that work engagement is related to productivity and profitability, but that it is most strongly related to client satisfaction measures.

Sources: Gutermann, D., N. Lehmann-Willenbrock, D. Boer, M. Born, and S.C. Voelpel (2016a), *Why Engaged Leaders Have Engaged Employees: A Multilevel Study of Engagement, LMX, and Follower Performance.* Paper presented at the Annual Meeting of the Academy of Management (AOM), Anaheim, USA

Gutermann, D., N. Lehmann-Willenbrock, S.C. Voelpel, and M. Born (2016b). *Unit-level Work Engagement as a Key to Organizational Performance.* Paper presented at the Annual Meeting of the Academy of Management (AOM), Anaheim, USA.Harter, J.K., F.L. Schmidt and T.L. Hayes (2002), "Business-unit-level relationships between employee satisfaction, employee engagement, and business outcomes: A meta-analysis", *Journal of Applied Psychology*, Vol. 87, pp. 268-279.

The development of a senior civil service (SCS), which is generally selected and developed through centralised programmes and managed as a whole across agencies, is a clear trend in OECD countries. These groups of women and men work in positions of great influence, and bridge the political and the administrative spheres to achieve results in an efficient, effective and legal manner. They are expected to develop and support their organisations and teams in achieving organisational objectives, and align the organisation with its environment (van Wart, 2003). They are also in a position to influence the organisational culture and values, and, under certain conditions, they can have a positive effect on the performance, motivation and satisfaction of their teams (Orazi et al., 2013). In all of the surveys and case studies discussed above, leadership is clearly identified as a driving force of engagement related outcomes.

Figure 3.8. The use of separate practices for the management of senior civil servants (2010 and 2016)

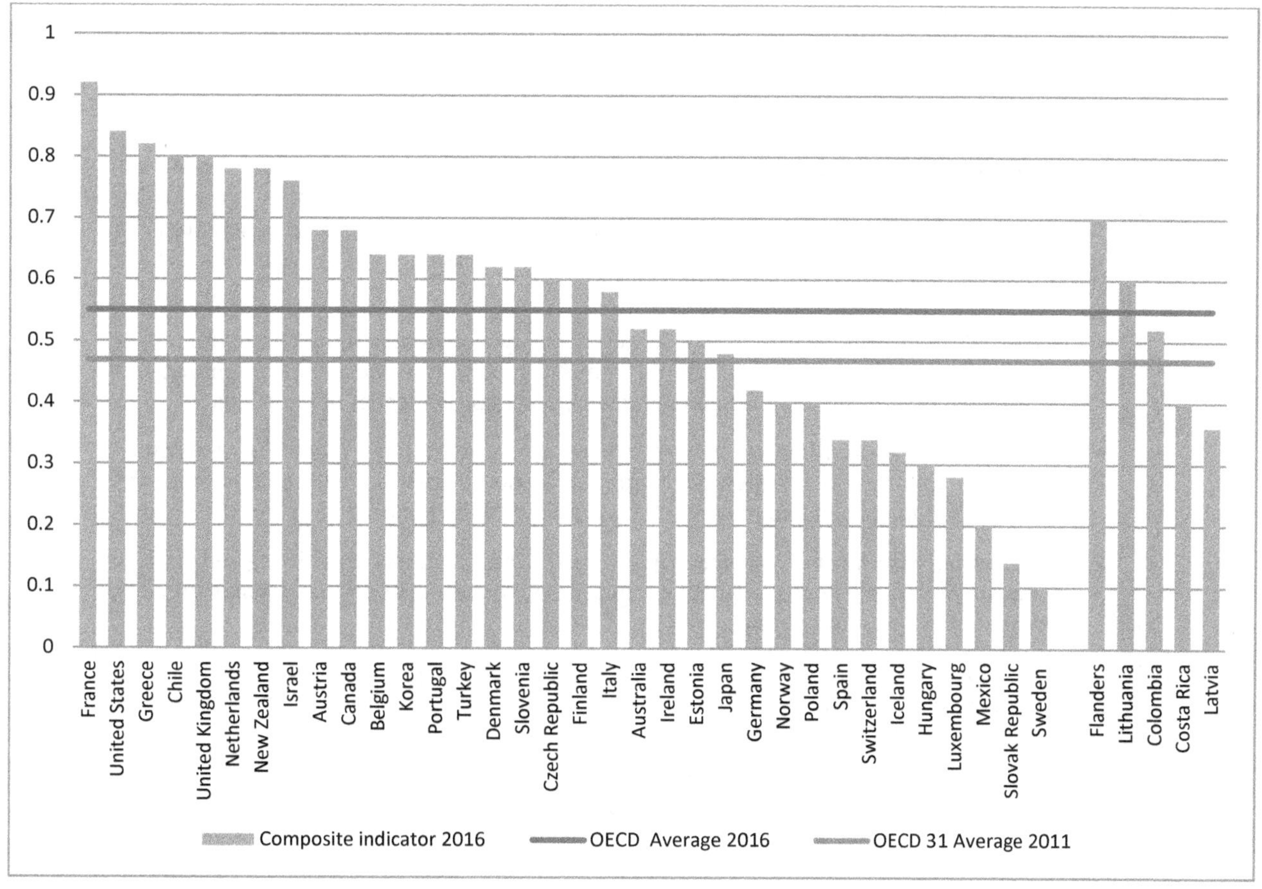

Source: OECD (2016), *Survey on Strategic Human Resources Management in Central/Federal Governments of OECD Countries*, OECD, Paris.

Expectations around the SCS role in organisations raise the question of what is organisational leadership in the public sector and what kind of leadership is required to support engagement. Leadership can be defined as a complex set of dynamic processes as change in the organisational environment calls for new types of leadership, and leaders are expected to be able to adapt and use new skills (van Wart, 2013).

One dominant strand of discussion related to leadership competencies questions whether transactional leadership should be replaced by transformational leadership, or whether, if necessary, both "leadership models" promise more success in the long term. In general, transactional leadership refers to leadership over goals, the setting of targets, alignment of resources to meet targets, incentives, etc. There usually remains an objective exchange relationship between management and employees (see Burns, 1978).

In contrast, transformational leadership, or emotional, charismatic or inspirational leadership, addresses the emotional level of those being led. The objective of transformational leadership is to build respect, trust and loyalty in a mutual leadership relationship. Employees are respected as people and not just professional service providers. For example, the University of St. Gallen's 2012 Leadership Conference changed its motto from "War for Talents" to "War for Hearts" in recognition that successful leadership must inspire and motivate, to attract and retain top quality employees.

Box 3.11. From transactional to transformational leadership and beyond

According to Bass (1985, 1997) the transactional-transformational leadership paradigm is a proven universal phenomenon in all cultures. At its most basic, leaders and followers enter into an exchange through a process of negotiation. Leaders then reward or punish followers depending on the level and quality of their achievements. This is transactional leadership. Transformational leadership recognizes the role of motivation and human emotion in the leader-follower relationship. "Authentic transformational leaders motivate followers to work for transcendental goals that go beyond immediate self-interests" (Bass, 1997). Bass identifies the following components of transformational leadership:

- **Idealised Influence** (Charisma) - leaders display conviction; emphasise trust; take stands on difficult issues; present their most important values; and emphasize the importance of purpose, commitment, and the ethical consequences of decisions.
- **Inspirational Motivation** - leaders articulate an appealing vision of the future, challenge followers with high standards, talk optimistically with enthusiasm, and provide encouragement and meaning for what needs to be done.
- **Intellectual Stimulation** - leaders question old assumptions, traditions, and beliefs; stimulate in others new perspectives and ways of doing things; and encourage the expression of ideas and reasons.
- **Individualised Consideration** - leaders deal with others as individuals; consider their individual needs, abilities, and aspirations; listen attentively; further their development; advise; teach; and coach.

While the transactional – transformation paradigm appears to have dominated leadership discussions for the last years, researchers and observers are beginning to ask whether even transformational leadership is appropriate for the challenges facing the public sector today and in the future. Sorensen and Torfing (2015) suggest that collaborative innovation in the public sector requires a different kind of leadership and management. They argue that, "Transactional and transformational leadership continue to be important to ensure an efficient implementation of predefined goals through well-described bureaucratic practices, but they have limited value when it comes to rethinking goals and practices and changing the way that problems and challenges are reframed and new practices are designed, tested and adjusted." They point instead to the discussions and debates around 'adaptive' and 'pragmatic' leadership:

- **Adaptive leadership** aims to determine which public activities to maintain and which to adapt and transform. It then seeks to develop new practices by crafting and testing prototypes and by aligning people across an organisation in order to ensure effective execution and to facilitate the integration of new activities with old ones.
- **Pragmatic leadership** aims to transform the culture of public organisations in ways that enhance double loop learning and use existing tools to solve problems by changing established practices – including transformative learning that develops new metaphors and narratives that help frame what is difficult to comprehend, expand knowledge and toolboxes and change identities and roles.

Sources: Bass, B.M (1997), "Does the Transactional-Transformational Leadership Paradigm Transcend Organizational and National Boundaries?", *American Psychologist*, Vol. 52/2, pp. 130-139

Bass, B.M. (1985), *Leadership and performance beyond expectations*, Free Press, New York.

Sorenson, E. and J. Torfing (2015), "Enhancing Public Innovation through Collaboration, Leadership and New Public Governance", in Nicholls, A., J. Simon and M. Gabriel (eds), *New Frontiers in Social Innovation Research*, Palgrave Macmillan.

In practice, transformational approaches can provide an essential complement to transactional leadership. "Academic studies show that in the longer term transactional and transformational leadership are together the more promising path of success" (Judge and Piccolo, 2004).

The need for the right balance of leadership styles may be particularly important during times of HRM reforms, which break the psychological contract and threaten to impact engagement if handled poorly (see Box 3.12 for an example). Experience has shown that implementing effective and sustainable change requires managers to support the change processes and clearly and transparently communicate the contents of reform. In doing so, they become role models themselves. Leaders need to be effective and transparent change managers to address these challenges and maintain high levels of engagement during reforms. They need to show commitment to the organisation and engage their employees in dialogue to communicate the purpose of the reform and promote sustainable change. Lastly, they need to provide sustained support to their management team to manage psychological contracts, or develop new ones.

Box 3.12. Leading for engagement: Findings from the UK experience

While organisational hierarchies change over time, the metadata from the People Survey on team-level reports provides information that can link team-level results over time.

In 2014 and 2015, the Cabinet Office team linked team-level data from the 2011 to 2014 surveys to identify two types of teams: those that had maintained high levels of employee engagement or well-being over the timespan, and those that had seen substantial increases in the levels of employee engagement or well-being. Having identified these types of teams, case study interviews were undertaken with a selection of employees that represented the range of different activities in government (policy advice, corporate services, front-line service delivery, regulation, etc.). The results of these case study interviews identified eight common factors that support high or improved levels of employee engagement and wellbeing:

1. Leaders who are passionate, visible, collaborative and welcome feedback.
2. Prioritise feedback, involvement and consultation.
3. Encourage innovation and creativity.
4. Make time for frontline exposure.
5. Challenge negative behaviours.
6. Support flexible working approaches.
7. Build team spirit and create time for people to talk to each other.
8. Take action on People Survey results.

Source: UK Cabinet Office (2015), *Engagement and Wellbeing: Civil Service Success Stories*, Blog post from Cabinet Office Analysis and Insight Team, Cabinet Office, London, https://coanalysis.blog.gov.uk/2015/07/08/engagement-and-wellbeing-civil-service-success-stories/, (accessed October 2016).

Good reforms take the leadership role into consideration at the planning stages and can result in improved employee engagement scores. Both Canada and Germany's BA have found that organisations and units that undergo budget reductions can actually increase their employee engagement scores, compared to organisations whose funding remained stable. This is likely due to steps taken by management to increase communication and availability to support staff through transition.

It can be helpful to think of leadership skills within a model of four basic competency clusters. Depending on policy and personnel decisions, and the core competencies of an organisation, these basic competencies can be backed up with sub-competencies. The basis of a job profile can be built on these (see Figure 3.9). Specialist/method competencies and activity and implementation competence most closely mirror transactional leadership, whereas social/communication and personal competence most closely reflect transformational leadership styles. Personal competencies of a leader are especially important to facilitate the basis for emotional ties to the employer, as well as an attachment to the tasks of an employee and his/her engagement.

Figure 3.9. Cluster for competency framework

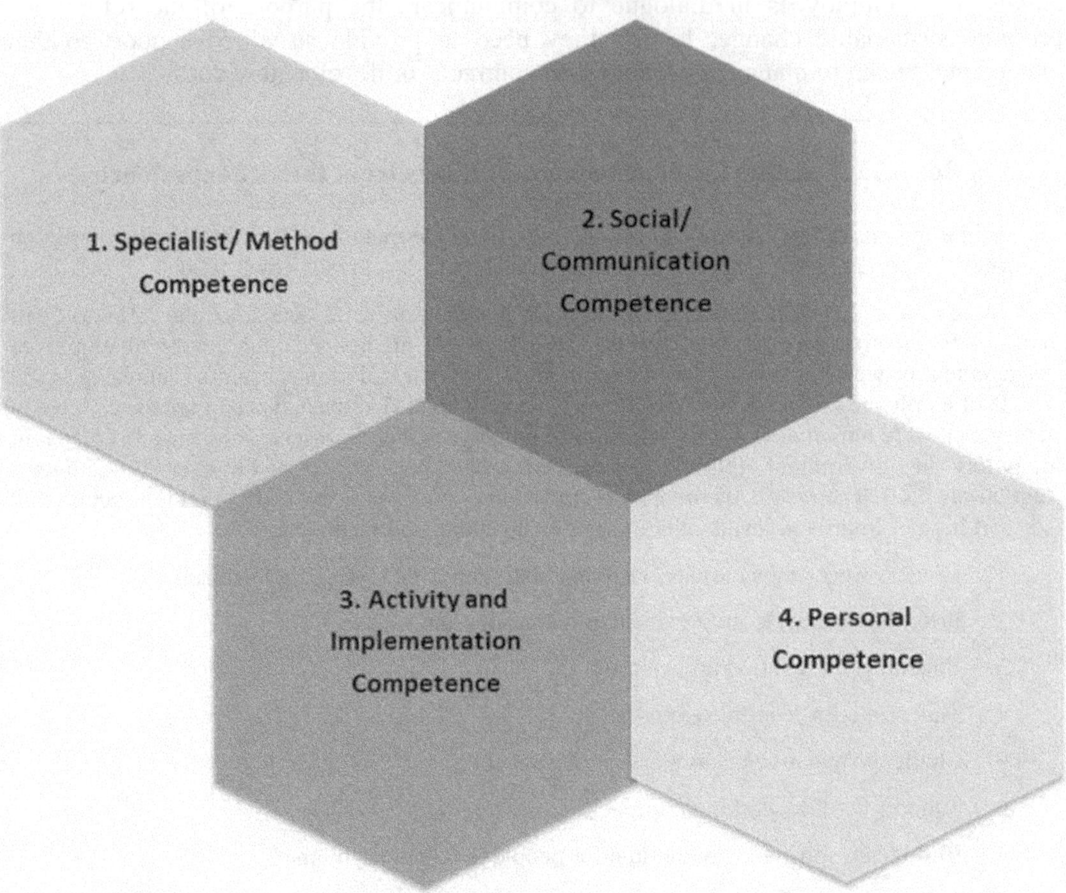

Source: Erpenbeck, J. and L. von Rosenstiel (eds.) (2003), Handbuch Kompetenzmessung: Erkennen, verstehen und bewerten von Kompetenzen in der betrieblichen, pädagogischen und psychologischen Praxis (2nd ed.) [Hanbook competency assessment – detecting, understanding and evaluating of competences in the occupational, educational and psychological practice], Schäffer-Poeschel, Stuttgart.

Recent data collected by the OECD on competencies priorities in the recruitment and development of senior managers indicates an increased awareness and shift towards transformational qualities of leadership. According to the 2016 SHRM survey, OECD countries prioritise people management, change management strategies, and values and ethics above traditionally transactional elements, such as financial management or technical specialisation.

Figure 3.10. Competencies prioritised when recruiting and developing senior managers (number of countries) (2016)

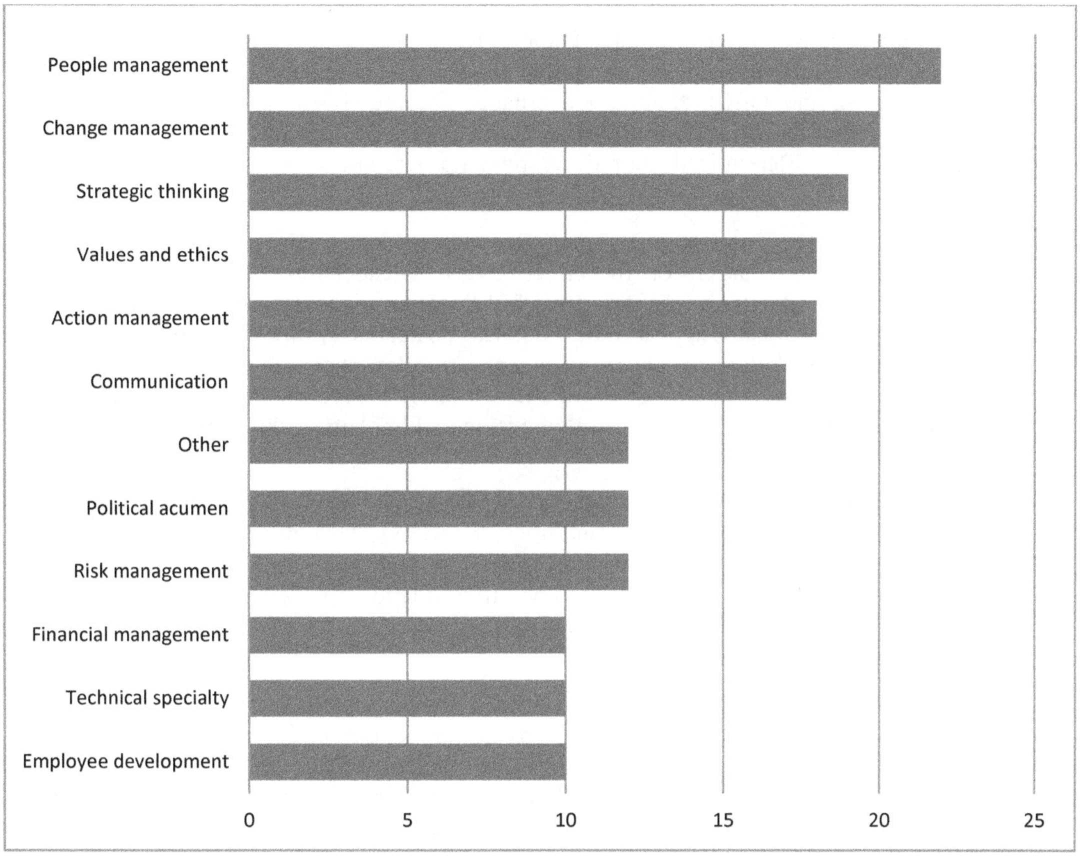

Source: OECD (2016), *Survey on Strategic Human Resources Management in Central/Federal Governments of OECD Countries*, OECD, Paris.

In Estonia, work to achieve a single government approach embeds the management of leadership competencies and staff engagement in an overall governmental approach (Box 3.13).

Box 3.13. Estonia's single government approach

One of the key priorities for Estonian public administration is to achieve better co-ordination across ministries and agencies for a *whole of government* approach to complex policy challenges. Besides changes in legislation, this also requires a change in organisational culture. The leaders of the public administration are being challenged to work in new ways to achieve a new level of co-operation and collaboration across the public administration, as well as between other stakeholders. Leadership plays a critical role in fostering the collaborative culture, as senior civil servants set an example to the rest of civil servants.

Meeting this challenge will require Estonia to prioritise new sets of top executive competencies. Based on analysis of the commitment survey of Estonian top civil servants (TNS Emor, 2011, 2014), the OECD Public Governance Review (OECD, 2011b), and annual performance assessments of top civil servants, Estonia has especially focused on three competencies to guide different leadership development programmes:

1. **Leadership**: The success of a single government approach, or any other goal or initiative, depends largely on the effectiveness of leadership. Latest research among senior civil servants (TNS Emor, 2011, 2014) shows high commitment of executives, while their subordinates appear to be much less dedicated. At the same time, main social competences, including people management, are often undervalued by top executives, despite their critical role in motivating the rest of civil servants. The effort they put into motivating their subordinates to own the vision and implement the common strategy has an impact on results.
2. **Co-operation and synergy**: A whole of government approach requires a wide spectrum of actors to work together in new and innovative ways. This means that leaders need to understand the broader context of the public service and show real commitment to collaboration and joint outcomes. Co-operation in Estonia's civil service often happens in a formalised way at a late stage, and is often perceived as a formal obligation rather than as a potential benefit.
3. **Innovative thinking**: In current financially challenging times, inspired and skilful leaders who can foster innovation and create new opportunities are needed. Estonia's approach to growing innovation begins by understanding where an individual or organisation is standing. For an executive, it is a matter of clarifying the situation before trying to develop a solution. This requires a better understanding of world trends and reasons behind them, as well as understanding local context. First, when looking at the Estonian Competency Framework, it requires better knowledge and skills of information processing to be able to find adequate information and to see "outside the box". Second, general skills of time-management and self-management are needed to be able to find more time for dealing with long-term issues rather than countless details of everyday activities. Third, it demands critical thinking to make a systematic evaluation and define the present need. Unconventional thinking and openness are important preconditions for innovative thinking.

Box 3.13. Estonia's single government approach *(continued)*

Figure 3.11. Competency framework of Estonian top civil servants (2009)

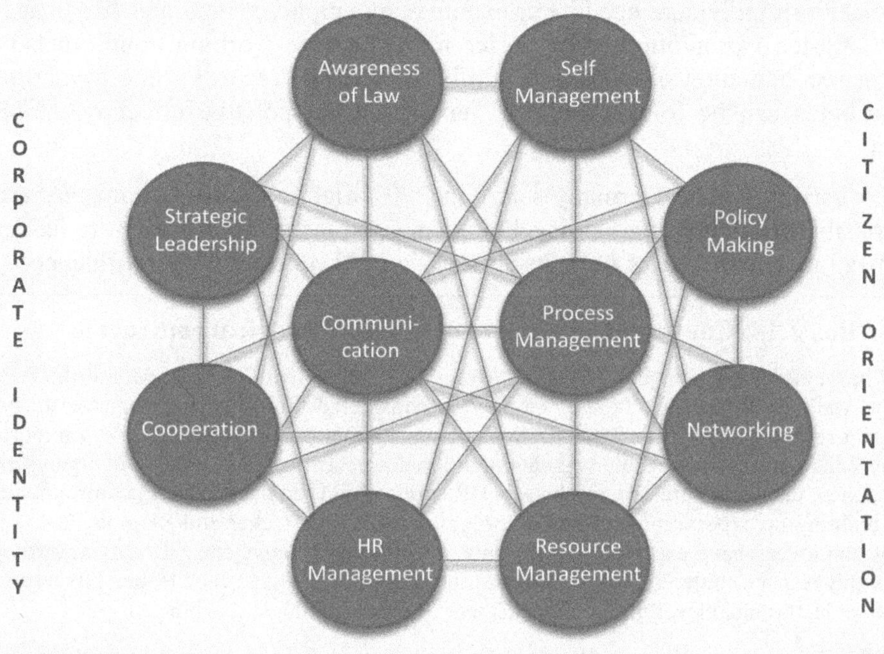

In order to enhance the *whole of government* approach and to increase the *government as enabler* mentality in Estonian public service and especially among top civil servants, several developmental programmes have been designed, implemented or are planned for the near future:

- Joint development programme *Innovation Needs Government, Government Needs Innovation* for Estonian and Finnish Public Service Top Executives to develop innovation capacity *(2015)*.
- Executive Development Programme for Deputy Directors and Heads of Regional Offices of Estonian Government Agencies to prepare the next round of top executives of Estonian Civil Service (2013).
- Policy-making programme for Deputy Secretary Generals to enhance the ability of leading the process of policy-making (planned for 2018).
- Talent Management Programme *Newton* for middle managers in public sector and Fast-Track Programme for university graduates to develop leadership competencies of the potential future leaders (since 2007).

Sources: Provided by the Government Office of Estonia: Commitment Survey of Estonian Top Civil Servants (TNS Emor & Government Office of Estonia, 2011,2014).

OECD (2011b), *Estonia: Towards a Single Government Approach*, OECD Public Governance Reviews, OECD Publishing, Paris, http://dx.doi.org/10.1787/9789264104860-en. v

Promoting employee engagement through HRM policies

A nuanced understanding of the different roles played by top leadership and direct managers can help inform employee engagement policies and address the psychological contract. However, managers and leaders will require access to a differentiated HRM-portfolio of tools to be able to address individual motives and needs of employees. An increasingly diverse workforce, with employees in different life-phases, requires a variety of HR policies to fit individual needs. For example, an employee in a later life-phase may not expect long-term promotions, but prefer more flexible working conditions, health promotion or reconciliation of work and family. If a "deal" regarding the psychological contract attributes can be found, this will have a strong positive effect on employee engagement.

Research carried out by Germany's BA in 2007 highlighted that managers are not solely responsible for upholding the psychological contract, but that the entire leadership of an organisation, and the HRM policies and services, have a significant influence.

Box 3.14. Contractual partners of the psychological contract

A 2007 survey of approximately 1 100 employees and their direct line managers at the German Employment Agency showed that 34% of employees considered the direct line manager to be the most important representative of the organisation. Managers themselves rated their own importance even higher. What was also noticeable was that additional aspects, such as signals via organisational culture and policy, team structure, the employer's HR services and top management, contribute just as strongly to building up expectations in the psychological contract (Hecker and Behrens, 2013). This showed that employees have expectations not only towards their managers, but also towards their employer. In this respect, strategies, HR services, structures, processes and each leadership system are important on an institutional level for the management of the psychological contract.

Figure 3.12. Two perspectives on the contractual partners of the psychological contract

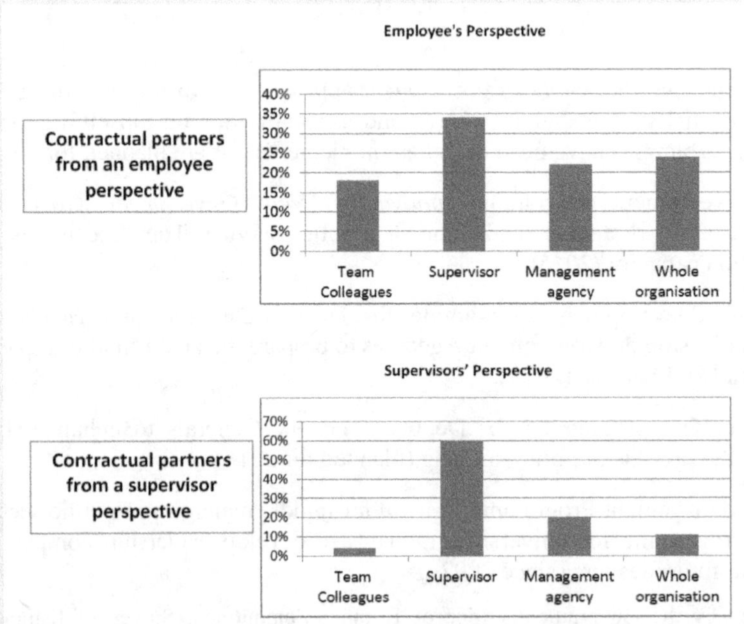

Sources: Hecker. D. (2010), "Merkmale psychologischer Verträge zwischen Beschäftigten und Organisationen" [Characteristics of psychological contracts between employees and organisations, dissertation, Friedrich-Alexander-University Erlangen-Nürnberg, p.150. Hecker, D. and B. Behrens, (2013), "Der psychologische Vertrag bei Veränderungsprozessen-Herausforderungen meistern" (The psychological contract during processes of change – Mastering challenges) (pp.103-118), in "Arbeitnehmer in Restrukturierungen: Gesundheit und Kompetenz erhalten" (Employees in restructuring measures: Maintaining health and competency), Federal Institute for Occupational Safety and Health, Bertelsmann, Bielefeld.

The country case studies and research confirm that employee engagement depends not only on personal relationships, but also on a range of HRM-related enablers and organisational development policies and strategies. The following figure is one model that shows how HRM functions and measures can be brought together to enhance employee well-being and employee performance (Guest, 2015). It is essential to answer the question of why employees should be engaged if HR policies are poor and demotivating, and organisations offer employees "nothing in return" (Guest, 2014: Figure 7).

Figure 3.13. The high commitment/engagement model of HRM and performance

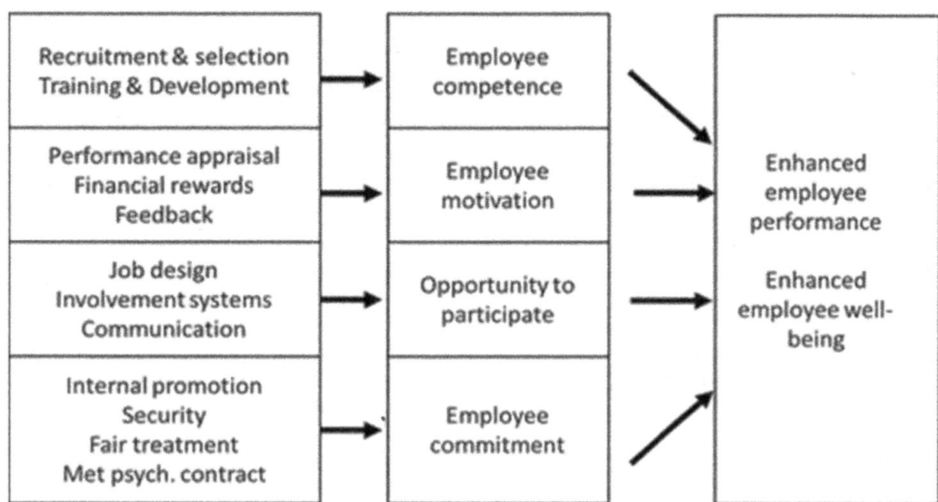

Source: Guest, D. (2015), *Employee Engagement: A Path to Organisational Success* (p.24), presentation made at the Lead, Engage, Perform expert meeting on public sector leadership, OECD, Paris, http://de.slideshare.net/OECD-GOV/david-guest-lead-engage-perform-oecd-21012015.

Working conditions and well-being

Discussions on the topic of well-being in the workplace are increasingly pointing to HR policies and programmes on, for example, working conditions and work organisation, dealing with stress and promoting resilience, good leadership and collaboration, work-life balance, and reconciliation of work and family, as well as flexible working time models from a life cycle perspective. Depending on the circumstances, these can either support or hinder engagement, creativity, capacity for innovation and service-oriented actions.. Supporting engagement, performance and capacity therefore implies a role for HRM beyond administering staff and managing costs. The main purpose of HRM strategies and policies is to promote organisational success in the future and to ensure that staff are healthy both emotionally and physically to contribute their fullest to the organisations' goals and values.

Foresight in HRM

HRM also has an important role to play as a business partner in planning for the future with foresight, and responding to future needs, risks and challenges within the organisation. This may require building strategic and conceptual competencies within HRM to establish future-oriented HRM policies and ensure that leaders see HRM as a necessary partner to achieving their organisational goals. This requires HR reforms that are well designed and resourced and that have a long-term view, as changing and reshaping organisational culture takes time.

HRM plays an important role as a business partner in supporting leaders during the phase of implementation and the follow-up of an employee survey. This requires well-trained HRM staff who are well prepared for their assignments. The Flemish "credo" from their example (Box 3.15) is that: "numbers need to be converted into action".

Box 3.15. Helping HRM business partners to align employee engagement studies with HR strategy

The Flemish Public Service organises an (non-mandatory) employee engagement survey every two years. Up until the 2014 edition of the survey participating entities received an (offline) entity-report and a global report on Flemish Public Service results. In the 2016 edition entities and global HR policy makers also have access to an experimental online reporting tool to make their own reports and additional analyses. Workshops for HR business partners, HR specialists and global HR policy makers are provided by the project team, assisting them to interpret the results, align the outcomes of the study with the HR strategy, and engage both employees and management in converting the outcomes into actions.

The workshop consists of four different parts. The first focuses on a few important issues concerning the interpretation of the reporting. Following this, participants are shown how to make their own reports and additional analyses with the experimental online reporting tool, with a specific focus on the important issues identified in the first part.

The third part focuses on getting the management summary right: what do the numbers and graphs "say", independently of the strategy. The focus is on benchmarking employee engagement on different levels: benchmarking is provided by age groups, gender, organisational entity and by a general mean of all participating entities. Also a benchmark is provided over time, so the evolution on different items becomes apparent. These benchmarks are supported by statistical methods e.g. confidence intervals and box plot methods.

Consequently, focus shifts to HR strategy to deduct which items in the engagement study are most important for a particular organisation and set targets for those items. The project team advises HR professionals to add more metrics from other surveys in the organisation and analyse hard data to enrich the numbers. In that way a pattern can become clear, and the metrics can provide real insights in the organisation. A template is made available for plotting targets against obtained results.

In the last part methods are discussed for engaging both employees and managers for converting numbers into actions. This includes discussion of different roles and the importance of a broad communication and follow-up. Overall, the importance of a long term perspective is stressed throughout the workshop: integrating employee engagement studies in defining HR and organisational targets, using them in benchmarking the evolution and further organisational development. This also assists in meaningful communication and avoiding a one-shot approach that may be more harmful then helpful.

The workshops and the use of the experimental online reporting tool will be evaluated thoroughly to ensure that the approach helps HR professionals in the Flemish government to take up their role of HR business partners even better. The Flemish HR agency believes the workshops will contribute to the goal of linking HR data with business challenges to build evidence on what benefits are connected to leveraging employee engagement studies. The agency aims to integrate this perception-data, adding more meaningful variables if necessary, with hard HR and organisation data (e.g. illness levels, exit rates) in the next edition (2018).

Source: provided to the OECD by the Flemish Government.

Changing demographics and the increasing diversity of staff is a good example of the need for flexible and future-oriented approaches to HRM. Internal surveys show that a diverse workforce places multiple and differentiated expectations on its employer in areas such as: value orientation, recognition and appreciation, working conditions, reconciliation of work and family, career opportunities, learning, and compensation. A one-size-fits-all approach to HRM is bound to fall short of meeting these expectations.

Holistic HRM

Lifecycle approaches in HRM that include gender and diversity issues (i.e. age), lifelong learning, knowledge management, well-being and motivation may be increasingly required to deliver services to employees and leaders effectively and efficiently. One practical example of an HR strategy in a public agency that brings many of these themes together is Germany's BA, which in 2010 and 2011 received awards from the American Association of Retired Persons (AARP) for its demographic-sensitive HRM strategy and practices that focus on the ageing workforce. Employee engagement is embedded in this approach to promote staff members' workability (competence, health, and engagement) (Box 3.16).

Box 3.16. The lifecycle oriented HRM policy of the German Employment Agency

The lifecycle oriented HR policy of Germany's BA is an intergenerational approach that seeks to enhance the workability of its staff and that focuses on competencies, health and engagement to promote lifelong learning and well-being in the workplace. Requirements to promote lifelong learning also support all measures of fostering sustainable change and innovation. The policy is embedded in an overall strategy to deliver customer-oriented services effectively and efficiently. With this policy, BA pursues a strategy that has high flexibility and the best possible reconciliation of work and private life in comparison with employer interests. The promotion of equal opportunity and gender mainstreaming are also included.

As a result, 61% of employees rated their personal reconciliation of work and private life in an internal survey as good or very good. For almost 80% of staff, equal opportunity policies are very important. Services and tools in BA's intergenerational management approach deliberately target employees at the beginning, in the middle, and at the end of their professional careers, and beyond. BA considers this policy, which includes corporate health management and knowledge management, as providing significant leverage to enhancing engagement and motivation, which is known to have a high correlation with customer satisfaction and individual and organisational performance.

Specific measures to bring organisational and individual needs together include: flexible working arrangements, such as part-time, mobile working, and teleworking; a family service to support employees in organising child care and care of relatives; on-the-job training; and a job-re-entry programme after long periods of absence following parental leave.

Source: Information provided by the German Employment Agency.

In the future, holistic approaches and the individualisation of HRM will play an increasingly significant role, as all HRM functions, such as recruiting, training, HRM development, HRM policies and compensation, can be oriented towards a common goal. Strategies are needed to promote the workability of staff to foster organisational performance. In this context, the Australian Public Service has developed a Capital

Planning Framework that includes people strategies and a variety of different policies (Figure 3.14).

Figure 3.14. APS Human Capital Planning Framework

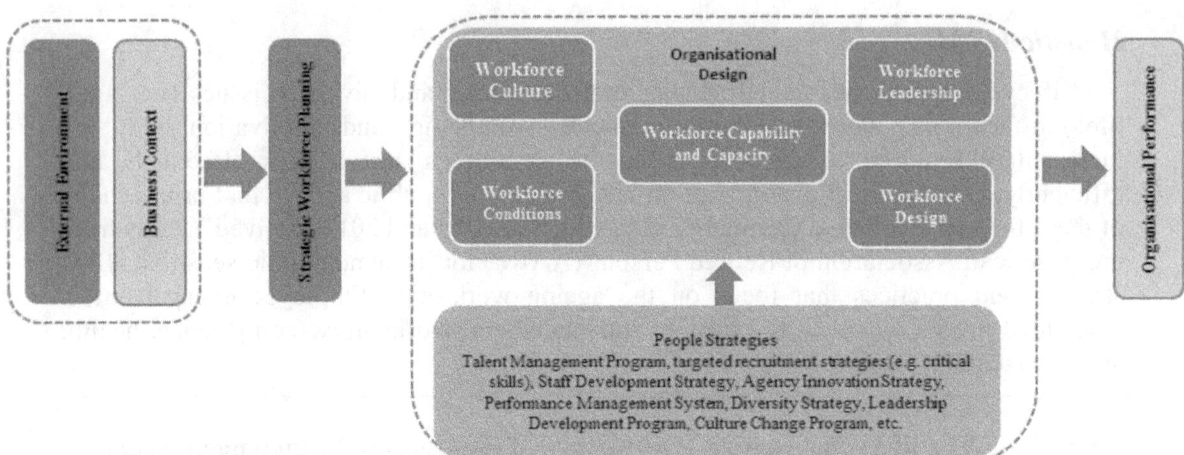

Source: Australian Public Service Commission (2012), *Human Capital Planning Framework*, Australian Public Service Commission Staff Research Insights, Canberra, http://www.apsc.gov.au/publications-and-media/current-publications/staff-research-insights/planning-framework.

A holistic framework could promote the implementation of an engagement approach in any organisation, and is also essential for an effective follow-up process. They help to contextualise and understand survey results, which deliver a good overview of the overall situation in the organisation or specific units. To reach the individual level and the specific individual relationship between employee and the leader, dialogue-based instruments can support this process to successfully manage change and shape a culture of trust and appreciation.

When considering the numerous enablers of employee engagement and trust, a holistic and strategic framework based on empirical evidence can help support leadership, management and HRM, and clarify their mutually supportive roles. Leaders shape organisational culture and manage adaptive change. Line managers need to manage individual relationships and psychological contracts. Both need support by dialogue-based leadership instruments, innovative HR policies and transparent information in order to be strong representatives of their organisation and its reforms.

Attracting the right talent to build the workforce of the future

In times of scarce financial resources and increasing demands of the public, modern public administration is expected to deliver citizen-oriented services effectively and efficiently, thus creating public value for modern societies. While civil services in many OECD countries are becoming smaller and leaner, they remain essential for the effective operation of governments. Attracting and recruiting the right kind of new talent will be essential to ensuring capacity in the long term.

In their effort to recruit talented staff equipped with the required skills, competencies and mindsets, public administrations come across many challanges:

- Although the number of public employees is not increasing, countries must cope with the challenge of critical skills shortages and the need for new talent at the right time.
- Payment and compensation in the public sector are often not competitive with the private sector, particularly for the highly competitive skillsets required in, for example, IT and STEM professions, commercial skills and managers of complex projects (e.g. infrastructure).
- Due to the impact of the demographic change, a large portion of employees will soon retire. Some countries face a shortage of skilled labour following low birth rates in past decades. Even the private sector is threatened, as this may be the biggest obstacle to growth, productivity and innovation.
- The image of the public sector as an employer may be decreasing in the perception of citizens, the media and potential applicants. Public administrations struggle with declining levels of trust among their citizens, as well as trust of their employees in good leadership and HR policies. HRM practice, including recruiting, may by slow and regarded as old fashioned, which may deter high quality applicants.

Research on recent graduates (sometimes known as Generation Y or millennials, i.e. those born between approximately 1977 and 2001) suggests that the newest generation of applicants and employees appears to be less attracted by the promise of working for the same employer their whole career. This generation has a clear vision and targets for their professional career and the willingness to work hard, but expects work-life balance, some autonomy in their working life, and that their work has a direct impact (see Domsch and Ladwig, 2015). This generation appears to have strong civic values and a high level of public service motivation. The question is whether or not government organisations are equipped to compete for their talents.

Multiple studies in various countries[3] suggest that this group is attracted by: opportunities for development and growth, quality of the working environment (positive environment, recognition of performance, management support), quality of the work assignments (variety, opportunity to contribute to improvement), and the reconciliation of work and family life. Providing attractive development programmes for top graduates that combine on the job learning, further education and real career development opportunities may be one way to appeal to the interests of Generation Y. Teleworking or mobile working, as well as flexible working arrangements, are increasingly sought after by the younger generation, and may go hand in hand with changing IT-supported workflows and services. Alternative working conditions may also be attractive for women who would like to work in leading positions and who want to have a family at the same time.

The decision to leave an employer is not always influenced by compensation. Leadership, work design and working conditions, engagement and a good relationship among colleagues are increasingly significant evidence-based predictors that make a valuable contribution to design retention programs (Allen, Bryant and Vardaman, 2010). The opportunity of lifelong learning is also being favoured as individual professional and life planning patterns are changing (modularisation in training and education).

By improving engagement through better leadership and management, and more flexible and individualised HRM, public organisations can create the conditions to attract and retain the right kind of talent to build the public workforce needed in the future. Improving engagement also allows managers to better tailor the psychological contract in line with new expectations and values. However, making these changes and building this kind of organisation requires a concerted communication effort. The US-based Partnership for Public Service brings together engagement related evidence and high-profile communication to annually identify the "best places to work" in the US federal government (Box 3.17).

Box 3.17. US Partnership for Public Service: Best places to work

The **Partnership for Public Service** is a unique non-partisan, non-profit organisation dedicated to achieving a more effective and innovative government for the United States. Employee satisfaction and commitment are two necessary ingredients in developing high-performing organisations and attracting top talent.

Since the first Best Places to Work in the Federal Government® rankings were released in 2003, they have provided managers and leaders with a way to measure and improve employee satisfaction and commitment, and are an important tool for ensuring that employee satisfaction is a top priority. They provide a mechanism for holding agency leaders accountable for the health of their organisations; serve as an early warning sign for agencies in trouble; and offer a roadmap for improvement.

The rankings also address one of the biggest barriers to federal employment: a lack of cross-governmental information for prospective employees. They provide job seekers unprecedented insight into opportunities for public service by highlighting the federal government's high-performing agencies and by promoting federal organisations that often go unheralded.

The 2015 Best Places to Work rankings include the views of more than 433 300 civil servants from **391 federal organisations** on a wide range of workplace topics. This includes the views of more than 421 700 employees who complete the US Office of Personnel Management's **Federal Employee Viewpoint Survey,** and employees from nine agencies, such as the Peace Corps, Smithsonian and the intelligence community who complete surveys with comparable questions.

Participating federal organisations are ranked according to overall employee satisfaction and commitment, as well as on 10 additional **categories,** such as leadership, strategic management, innovation and work–life balance. The organisations are also ranked using data from **demographic** and **occupational** groupings.

In addition to the rankings, the website provides an overview of each agency and subcomponent, trend data and expert analysis of what the results mean. Users can conduct side-by-side comparisons of how agencies or their subcomponents rank in various categories, how they compare with other agencies and determine whether they have improved or regressed over time.

For the first time, 75 federal organisations have been grouped by mission into six areas: public health, law enforcement, national security, energy and environment, financial regulation and oversight. The data show a wide range of scores among agencies with similar workforces and responsibilities.

Source: Partnership for Public Service (2016), *Webpage of the best places to work in the federal government*, Partnership for Public Service, New York, http://bestplacestowork.org/BPTW/index.php. (accessed October 2016).

Employer branding in the public sector

"An employer brand is a collection of ideas and beliefs that influence the way current and potential employees view an organisation and the employment experience that organisation is offering. It communicates the company's culture and values and helps to ensure employees are passionate about, and fit in with, the organisational culture to help move the company forward" (Parmar, 2014: 202). An employer branding strategy, therefore, is much more than HR marketing and the distribution of flyers or brochures. It needs to work on culture and staff engagement within a holistic HRM approach that is embedded in an overall corporate strategy.

The main challenge of employer branding in the public sector is to shape public administration's image as a high performance service provider and an attractive, trustworthy and credible employer. The public sector can strengthen its brand by emphasising a focus on high quality, customer orientation and public value. Citizens or customers are often not aware of what a public administration is capable of doing to serve societal needs. Negative headlines in the news can leave a lasting negative impact.

Public sector workers create the image of a modern administration in the public mind mainly through their dedication and commitment to their work. Engaged staff convey these ideals and values to the public more effectively and consistently than disengaged employees and leaders. Together, they have great potential to influence the service climate and build trust in public administration (see Heintzman and Marson, 2005; Salanova, Agut and Peiro, 2005). A strong identification with their employer, and even a sense of pride, are important factors, particular when dealing directly with citizens. Their appearance in public and the way they report about their employers, their leaders, management and colleagues in social media is increasingly relevant.

Engaged employees can also have a positive impact on attracting prospective employees, as they will readily recommend their employer to others when the conditions are right. This can have a positive effect in terms of recruiting high demand skills in times of high retirement and public service reforms.

Organisational or governmental employer branding is, therefore, an integral part of an effective HR strategy. Within each public administration, a discussion is needed of what makes the public administration an attractive employer and what could be done to build on these. Attractive working conditions, interesting jobs, and training opportunities need to be considered alongside pay and benefits. Individual approaches for each agency/organisation may benefit from an overall governmental approach. Each agency may be different in terms of culture, tasks and daily challenges, development paths, reform history, and public perceptions. Data from surveys can be helpful to develop evidence-based policies to support tailor-made strategies.

Policy lessons for a more engaged civil service

Chapter 2 of this report showed that the pressure on central public administrations (CPAs) to become leaner and reduce costs has required many OECD countries to make cuts that have likely resulted in negative impacts on the workforce regarding trust, motivation and commitment. This threatens to erode longer-term capacity in terms of workforce productivity, attraction of skills needed to create public value, and the future innovative potential of the workforce. Looking forward, the question is not how big or small should the workforce be, but what kind of employee is required to meet the challenges facing public administrations today and into the future. If CPAs are to become and remain leaner, countries cannot afford to have employees who are not ready to commit their full selves and skillsets to solving the complex challenges that define today's public sector work. In short, countries cannot afford to have unengaged employees. Countries need to invest in the conditions that create engagement to secure the future capacity of their workforce and, by extension, government.

The most comprehensive study to date on the impact of employee engagement on productivity and innovation was carried out in the United Kingdom. At the end of the report it is noted that "Despite there being some debate about the precise meaning of employee engagement there are three things we know about it: it is measurable; it can be correlated with performance; and it varies from poor to great." (MacLeod and Clarke, 2011: 10).

Academic and practical discourse on almost 50 definitions of engagement and different scales of measurement persist. The examples presented in this report show that depending on strategic, political and intercultural factors, engagement can be measured and defined in very different ways (and some countries may choose to call it something else entirely). Conceptualisations of engagement vary, different measurement indices may group different sets of perceptions, and different follow-up processes are used to try to move from measurement to management.

What is common across the cases presented in this report is that civil services are developing increasingly evidence-based and data-driven approaches to identifying management strengths and weaknesses, improving leadership and better targeting HRM reforms and strategies. Regardless of the details of the engagement index, some civil services are making concerted efforts to take employee's viewpoints into consideration and recognise that the perception of the workforce matters for attraction and retention, productivity and innovation. This should be seen as an essential counterbalance to the austerity-oriented measures profiled in the first part of this report, and as a central element of all HRM and leadership strategies, which aim to secure the future capacity of OECD civil services to be a positive force in the lives of the citizens they serve.

Engagement has primarily positive connotations, but can also be understood in a negative sense if it appears that employees are being asked to improve their attitude and performance without receiving anything in return. The analysis in this report reinforces the notion that engagement is not only the responsibility of the individual employee, but also that of the employer, who is the driving force responsible for designing the right working conditions that lead to better engagement. This implies that engagement models should be embedded in a holistic HRM model with leadership and working conditions to foster engagement and measures to evaluate the effects and success. Engagement should be a factor of consideration in all HRM reforms, whether intended to cut size and costs or increase employer attractiveness.

While it is early days for the kind of evidence-driven HRM that is presented and promoted in this report, some common practices can be gleaned from the cases and the literature that appear to have promising results. For example, the leading practices in the area of engagement seem to include the following:

- Regular employee surveys, which are designed around an engagement model/theory, to measure engagement and its drivers. Surveys are generally cross-departmental and, ideally, civil-service wide, to enable comparative analysis and benchmarking across and within organisations. Conducting the survey at regular intervals enables trends analysis, which is essential to detect improvements over time.

- Custom reports to managers benchmarking their unit's scores against similar units, their organisation, and the civil service average. These reports enable the manager to see year-over-year trends, and to locate their score within a broader context. It is also important that benchmarks are produced for key performance indicators (e.g. engagement index) and contextual factors that may influence the Key Performance Indicators to give indications of follow up mechanisms.
- Follow-up processes owned by the individual managers, with some centralised specialist support. It is important that each manager accepts the responsibility to respond to their survey scores. Successful responses profiled in this report that have led to an improvement of scores generally appear to have the following components:
  - **Clear commitment from the top leadership of the organisation**. Top leadership clearly communicates to all staff that engagement is a priority, that survey results will be used to make changes, and that later surveys will be used to hold leadership accountable for delivering results.
  - **Improved communication**. Whether in the form of face-to-face town hall meetings and/or online social networks, organisations who have successfully improved their engagement scores appear to have developed multiple channels for staff to communicate with senior managers, and vice versa.
  - **Meaningful contribution to improvements**. Most successful organisations have put into place processes that enable staff to actively contribute ideas to the improvement of their workplaces and organisational culture.
  - **Support to managers**. Managers can benefit from initial support from the survey authority to understand and interpret their results. The quality of the personal relationship between employees and their direct supervisors appears to have a significant impact on engagement. Successful organisations have supported middle managers to develop action plans that improve these relationships. Support could come in the form of toolkits, including HRM tools to negotiate working conditions, learning and development opportunities, and flexible arrangements that fit with individual employees' own needs and ambitions.
  - **Holistic and forward looking HRM policies, strategies and tools.** HRM needs to contribute more than HR transactions, numbers analysis and cost control. HRM policies can support employee wellbeing, development and performance at all stages of a lifecycle. HRM tools can support managers and leaders to ensure they are able to manage psychological contracts and support an engaged workforce. This includes good HR data, integrated planning process, and future oriented competency management.

An employee engagement strategy requires a targeted communication and information strategy, employee participation, and managers who support the concepts of promoting employee motivation and engagement. Experience in various OECD countries has shown that such actions can provide a powerful counterbalance to the austerity-driven measures outlined in the first part of this report. A loss of trust, as well as continuing tense circumstances, can be minimised in the long term only through transparent communication on an institutional and individual level. Even more compelling may be the preventative impacts of a focus on engagement; since organisations will likely weather change and transition better if they start with a high level of engagement from their workforce.

Employee engagement surveys are not an end unto themselves; but provide a basis for objective management discussions, data to adjust policies, incentives for organisations to improve and a way to communicate the importance of the employee to meeting organisational objectives. By focusing on aligning objectives, engagement conversations can also help make more explicit the changing challenges and pressures faced by the public sector, and the role of both employee and organisations to respond. This helps build ownership for some of the difficult decisions that will have to be made, and supports more agile and tailored HRM measures. Finally, a focus on engagement also enables organisations to understand what attracts, motivates and retains top-performing employees to ensure the public sector has the talent, skills and capacity to perform at the highest levels and meet citizens' increasingly complex needs and expectations.

Notes

1 https://www.fedview.opm.gov/2016FILES/2016_FEVS_Gwide_Final_Report.PDF.

2 See, for example, Risher (no date) for a good overview of the important role played by middle management in the US system.

3 See, for example:

- United States: Partnership for Public Service (2014), *College Students Are Attracted to Federal Service, but Agencies Need to Capitalize on Their Interest*, https://ourpublicservice.org/publications/download.php?id=20
- France: Institute of Public Management and Economic Development (2011), *Generation Y and Public Management: Issues and Implications*, http://www.economie.gouv.fr/files/pmo_38.pdf.
- Australia: Richard P. Winter and Brent A. Jackson (2016), "Work values preferences of Generation Y: performance relationship insights in the Australian Public Service", *The International Journal of Human Resource Management*, Vol. 27/17, http://dx.doi.org/10.1080/09585192.2015.1102161.

Notes

1. [illegible]

2. See, for example, Fisher ([illegible]) for a [illegible] of the important role played by [illegible] in the US system.

3. See, for example:

- United States Partnership for Public Service (2014), College Students [illegible] [illegible]
- France, Institut de la gestion publique et du développement économique (20[illegible]) [illegible]
- Vandenabeele, [illegible] and Brans, [illegible] (2010), [illegible]

References

Allen, D.G., P.C. Bryant and J.M. Vardaman (2010), "Retaining talent: replacing misconceptions with evidence-based strategies", *Academy of Management Perspectives*, Vol. 24, No. 2, pp. 48-64.

Australian Government (2016), *Dataset on employee census*, https://data.gov.au/dataset/aps-employee-census-2016, (accessed October 2016).

Bakker, A.B. (2011), "An evidence-based model of work engagement", *Current Directions in Psychological Science*, Vol. 20, No. 4, pp. 265-269.

Bakker, A.B. (2009), "Building engagement in the workplace", in Cooper, C.L. and R.J. Burke (eds.), *The peak performing organization*,, Routledge, Oxon, UK, pp. 50-72.

Bakker, A.B., E. Demerouti and A.I. Sanz-Vergel (2014), "Burnout and work engagement: The JD–R approach", *Annual Review of Organizational Psychology and Organizational Behavior*, Vol. 1, pp. 389-411.

Bass, B.M. (1997), "Does the Transactional-Transformational Leadership Paradigm Transcend Organizational and National Boundaries?", *American Psychologist*, Vol. 52/2, pp. 130-139.

Bass, B.M. (1985), *Leadership and performance beyond expectations,* Free Press, New York.

Burns, J.M. (1978), *Leadership*, New York, Harper & Row.

Domsch, M.E. and D.H. Ladwig (2015), "Erwartungen der Generation Y", *PERSONALquarterly*, Vol. 1, pp. 10-14.

Erpenbeck, J. and L. von Rosenstiel (eds.) (2003), *Handbuch Kompetenzmessung: Erkennen, verstehen und bewerten von Kompetenzen in der betrieblichen, pädagogischen und psychologischen Praxis* (2nd ed.) (Hanbook competency assessment – detecting, understanding and evaluating of competences in the occupational, educational and psychological practice), Schäffer-Poeschel, Stuttgart.

Guest, D. (2015), *Employee Engagement: A Path to Organisational Success,* presentation made at the Lead, Engage, Perform expert meeting on public sector leadership, OECD, Paris, http://de.slideshare.net/OECD-GOV/david-guest-lead-engage-perform-oecd-21012015.

Guest, D. (2014), "Employee engagement: a sceptical analysis", *Journal of Organizational Effectiveness: People and Performance*, Vol. 1, No. 2, pp. 141-156.

Guest, D. (2004), "The Psychology of the Employment Relationship: An Analysis Based on the Psychological Contract", *Applied Psychology: An International Review*, Vol. 53, No. 4, pp. 541-555.

Guest, D. and N. Conway (1997), *Employee Motivation and the Psychological Contract*, CIPD, London.

Gutermann, D., N. Lehmann-Willenbrock, D. Boer, M. Born, and S.C. Voelpel (2016a), *Why Engaged Leaders Have Engaged Employees: A Multilevel Study of Engagement, LMX, and Follower Performance*, Paper presented at the Annual Meeting of the Academy of Management (AOM), Anaheim, USA

Gutermann, D., N. Lehmann-Willenbrock, S.C. Voelpel, and M. Born (2016b), *Unit-level Work Engagement as a Key to Organizational Performance*, Paper presented at the Annual Meeting of the Academy of Management (AOM), Anaheim, USA.

Harter, J.K., F.L. Schmidt and T.L. Hayes (2002), "Business-unit-level relationships between employee satisfaction, employee engagement, and business outcomes: A meta-analysis", *Journal of Applied Psychology*, Vol. 87, pp. 268-279.

Hecker. D. (2010), "Merkmale psychologischer Verträge zwischen Beschäftigten und Organisationen" (Characteristics of psychological contracts between employees and organisations), dissertation, Friedrich-Alexander-University Erlangen-Nürnberg.

Hecker, D. and B. Behrens, (2013), "Der psychologische Vertrag bei Veränderungsprozessen- Herausforderungen meistern" (The psychological contract during processes of change – Mastering challenges) (pp.103-118), in the publication by the Federal Institute for Occupational Safety and Health, "Arbeitnehmer in Restrukturierungen: Gesundheit und Kompetenz erhalten" (Employees in restructuring measures: Maintaining health and competency), Bertelsmann, Bielefeld.

Heintzman, R. and B. Marson (2005), "People, service, trust: is there a public sector service value chain?", *International Review of Administrative Sciences*, Vol. 71, No. 4, pp. 549–575, http://ras.sagepub.com/content/71/4/549.

Iaffaldano, M.T. and P.M Muchinsky (1985), "Job satisfaction and job performance: A meta-analysis", *Psychological Bulletin*, Vol. 97, No. 2, pp. 251-273.

Institute of Public Management and Economic Development (2011), *Generation Y and Public Management: Issues and Implications*, http://www.economie.gouv.fr/files/pmo_38.pdf.

Johnson, J.L. and A.M. O'Leary-Kelly (2003), "The effects of psychological contract breach and organizational cynicism: not all social exchange violations are created equal", *Journal of Organizational Behavior*, Vol. 24, No. 5, pp. 627-647.

Judge, T.A. and R.F. Piccolo (2004), "Transformational and transactional leadership: A meta-analytic test of their relative validity", *Journal of Applied Psychology,* Vol. 89, pp. 755-768.

Judge, T.A., C.J. Thoresen, J.E. Bono and G.K. Patton (2001), "The job satisfaction - job performance relationship: A qualitative and quantitative review", *Psychological Bulletin,* Vol. 127, No.3, pp. 376-407.

MacLeod, D. and N. Clarke (2011), *Engaging for success: Enhancing performance through employee engagement – A report to the government,* Institute of Education, London, http://dera.ioe.ac.uk/1810/1/file52215.pdf.

Meynhardt, T. and S. Bartholomes (2011), "(De)Composing public value: in search of basic dimensions and common ground", *International Public Management Journal*, Vol. 14, No. 3, pp. 284-308.

OECD (2016), *Survey on Strategic Human Resources Management in Central/Federal Governments of OECD Countries*, OECD, Paris.

OECD (2014), *Survey on managing budgetary constraints: implications for HRM and employment in central public administration*, OECD, Paris, www.oecd.org/gov/pem/2014-human-resource-management-survey.pdf.

OECD (2011a), *Public Servants as Partners for growth: Towards a Stronger, Leaner and More Equitable Workforce*, OECD Publishing, Paris, DOI: http://dx.doi.org/10.1787/9789264166707-en

OECD (2011b), *Estonia: Towards a Single Government Approach*, OECD Public Governance Reviews, OECD Publishing, Paris, http://dx.doi.org/10.1787/9789264104860-en.

OPM (2015), *Federal Employee Viewpoint Survey Results: Employees Influencing Change,* Governmentwide Management Report, United States Office of Personnel Management, https://www.fedview.opm.gov/2016FILES/FEVS_Engagement_INFOGRAPHIC.pdf

Orazi, D.C., A. Turrini and G. Valotti (2013), "Public sector leadership: new perspectives for research and practice", *International Review of Administrative Sciences*, Vol. 79(3), pp. 486–504.

Parmar. A. (2014), "The Role of HR Department in Employer Branding at Public and Private Sector", *Journal of human Resources Management and Labor Studies*, Vol. 2, No 2, pp. 201-225.

Partnership for Public Service (2016), *Webpage of the best places to work in the federal government*, Partnership for Public Service, New York, http://bestplacestowork.org/BPTW/index.php, (accessed October 2016).

Parzefall, M.R. and J. Hakanen (2010), "Psychological contract and its motivational and health-enhancing properties", *Journal of Managerial Psychology*, Vol. 25, No. 1, pp. 4-21.

Petty, M.M., G.W. McGee and J.W. Cavender (1984), "A meta-analysis of the relationships between individual job satisfaction and individual performance", *The Academy of Management Review*, Vol. 9, No. 4, pp. 712-721.

Rich, B.L. (2006), *Job engagement: Construct validation and relationships with job satisfaction, job involvement, and intrinsic motivation,* Gainesville, University of Florida, http://www.gbv.de/dms/zbw/583845355.pdf

Rich, B.L., J.A. Lepine and E.R. Crawford (2010), "Job Engagement, Antecedents and Effects on Job Performance", *Academy of Management Journal*, Vol. 53, No. 3, pp. 617-635.

Rousseau, D.M. (1995), *Psychological contracts in organizations: Understanding written and unwritten agreements*, Sage, London.

Saks, A.M. and J.A. Gruman (2014), "What Do We Really Know About Employee Engagement?", *Human Resource Development Quaterly*, Vol. 25, No. 2, pp.155-182.

Salanova, M., S. Agut and J.M. Peiro (2005), "Linking Organisational Resources and Work Engagement to Employee Performance and Customer Loyalty; The Mediation of Service Climate", *Journal of Applied Psychology*, Vol. 90., No. 6, pp.1217-1227.

Salanova, M. and W.B. Schaufeli (2008), "Job resources, engagement and proactive behaviour", *International Journal of Human Resource Management*, Vol. 19, pp.116-131.

Schaufeli, W.B. and A.B. Bakker (2010), "Defining and measuring work engagement: Bringing clarity to the concept", in A.A. Bakker and M.P. Leiter (eds.), *Work Engagement - A Handbook of Essential Theory and Research* (pp.10-24), Psychology Press, New York.

Schaufeli, W.B. and A.B. Bakker (2004), "Job demands, job resources and their relationship with burnout and engagement: A multi-sample study", *Journal of Organizational Behavior*, Vol. 25, pp. 293-315.

Sonnentag, S., C. Binnewies and E.J. Mojza (2010), "Staying well and engaged when demands are high: the role of psychological detachment", *Journal of Applied Psychology*, Vol. 95, pp.965-976.

Sorenson, E. and J. Torfing (2015), "Enhancing Public Innovation through Collaboration, Leadership and New Public Governance", in Nicholls, A., J. Simon and M. Gabriel (eds), *New Frontiers in Social Innovation Research,* Palgrave Macmillan.

UK Cabinet Office (2015), *Engagement and Wellbeing: Civil Service Success Stories*, Blog post from Cabinet Office Analysis and Insight Team, Cabinet Office, London, https://coanalysis.blog.gov.uk/2015/07/08/engagement-and-wellbeing-civil-service-success-stories/, (accessed October 2016).

UK Cabinet Office (2013), *Civil Service People Survey*, Cabinet Office, London, http://webarchive.nationalarchives.gov.uk/20140305122816/http://resources.civilservice.gov.uk/wp-content/uploads/2014/02/csps2013_summary_of_findings.pdf.

van Wart, M. (2013), "Lessons from Leadership Theory and the Contemporary Challenges of Leaders", *Public Administration Review*, Vol. 73/4, pp. 553–565, DOI: 10.1111/puar.12069.

von Rosenstiel, L., W. Molt and B. Rüttinger (2005), *Organisationspsychologie* (9th completely revised and expanded ed.), Kohlhammer, Stuttgart.

Vroom, V.H. (1964), *Work and motivation*, Wiley, New York.

Winter, R.P. and B.A. Jackson (2016), "Work values preferences of Generation Y: performance relationship insights in the Australian Public Service", *The International Journal of Human Resource Management*, Vol. 27/17, http://dx.doi.org/10.1080/09585192.2015.1102161.

ORGANISATION FOR ECONOMIC CO-OPERATION AND DEVELOPMENT

The OECD is a unique forum where governments work together to address the economic, social and environmental challenges of globalisation. The OECD is also at the forefront of efforts to understand and to help governments respond to new developments and concerns, such as corporate governance, the information economy and the challenges of an ageing population. The Organisation provides a setting where governments can compare policy experiences, seek answers to common problems, identify good practice and work to co-ordinate domestic and international policies.

The OECD member countries are: Australia, Austria, Belgium, Canada, Chile, the Czech Republic, Denmark, Estonia, Finland, France, Germany, Greece, Hungary, Iceland, Ireland, Israel, Italy, Japan, Korea, Latvia, Luxembourg, Mexico, the Netherlands, New Zealand, Norway, Poland, Portugal, the Slovak Republic, Slovenia, Spain, Sweden, Switzerland, Turkey, the United Kingdom and the United States. The European Union takes part in the work of the OECD.

OECD Publishing disseminates widely the results of the Organisation's statistics gathering and research on economic, social and environmental issues, as well as the conventions, guidelines and standards agreed by its members.

OECD PUBLISHING, 2, rue André-Pascal, 75775 PARIS CEDEX 16
(42 2016 45 1 P) ISBN 978-92-64-26718-3 – 2016

www.ingramcontent.com/pod-product-compliance
Lightning Source LLC
LaVergne TN
LVHW081412110826
845149LV00010B/1715

* 9 7 8 9 2 6 4 2 6 7 1 8 3 *